Twayne's United States Authors Series

EDITOR OF THIS VOLUME

Kenneth E. Eble
University of Utah

Zora Neale Hurston

TUSAS 381

Zora Neale Hurston

ZORA NEALE HURSTON

By LILLIE P. HOWARD

Wright State University

TWAYNE PUBLISHERS

A DIVISION OF G. K. HALL & CO., BOSTON

Copyright © 1980 by G. K. Hall & Co.

Published in 1980 by Twayne Publishers,
A Division of G. K. Hall & Co.
All Rights Reserved

Printed on permanent/durable acid-free paper and bound
in the United States of America

First Printing

Library of Congress Cataloging in Publication Data

Howard, Lillie P
    Zora Neale Hurston.

    (Twayne's United States authors series ; TUSAS 381)
    Bibliography: p. 186
    Includes index.
    1. Hurston, Zora Neale—Criticism and interpretation.
PS3515.U789Z73   813'.52   80-24907
ISBN 0-8057-7296-0

Contents

About the Author

Lillie P. Howard became interested in Zora Hurston while working on her doctorate at the University of New Mexico. She wrote her dissertation—"Zora Neale Hurston: A Non-Revolutionary Black Artist"—on Hurston, and after completing her degree continued the research which led to this book. She is an associate professor of English at Wright State University, Dayton, Ohio, where she teaches English and American literature.

She has published in *CLA Journal, American Women Writers, Antioch Review, Harper's Weekly, Pulp Magazine, Callaloo,* and Wright State *University Times.*

Preface

For the past few years, students, critics, and friends have tried
to fathom the enigma known as Zora Neale Hurston. They will
continue to probe her mystery but I am convinced that no one
will ever produce a definitive Zora Hurston. The best one can
hope for is a reasonable fascimile thereof, a superior piecing
together of all the parts, the evidence. But one must always
remember that evidence sometimes lies (especially since Zora
herself, the provider of the evidence, often lied), that even when
it does not lie, it must be interpreted, that interpretations, gov-
erned as they are by the nature and limitations of our own
experiences, are subjective, that our images of Zora Neale Hurston will always be just that—ours.

We are left, then, with *our* Zora Neale Hurston—a woman
Fannie Hurst remembered as having existed "in bas relief, only
partially emerging from her potential into the whole woman."
We are left with memories of an effervescent and irridescent
personality, with an "individual of the greatest magnitude," with
a "short shelf of writings" that deserve "to endure." This book
aims, through close study of Hurston's works, to bring Hurston
out of "bas relief" as much as possible, recognizing, however, that
when all is said and done, Hurston will still be in the shadows
protecting herself as best she can from unwitting probers of the
substance of her life. In his biography, Robert Hemenway
humbly admits that the "definitive" book on Hurston remains to
be written. So it remains still. While Hemenway ambitiously
aimed to study a "literary artist of sufficient talent" who "deserved
intensive study" so as to give her "an important place in American
literary history," I attempt a critical analysis of her life and her
works, in order to help bring Zora to the favorable public notice
she has so long deserved. Chapters 1, 2, and 3 are devoted to
Hurston's life and times and her short works, while the remaining

chapters deal with her book-length works. One chapter is devoted to each piece of fiction, one chapter to the nonfiction.

I owe a large debt, of course, to Robert Hemenway for his support, his help and encouragement, his invaluable biography. Thanks also go to the librarians at the University of Florida, Yale University, and Howard University who assisted me with my research; to Everette Hurston, Zora's brother, for consenting to an interview and sharing a number of precious memories with me; to Stephen Haas and Joy Iddings of the Wright State University library who were unflagging in getting material for me. Special thanks to the College of Liberal Arts, Wright State University, whose much-needed grants made it possible for me to conduct my research; to my typist, Carol Chandler, who worked almost as hard as I did; and to the numerous students and friends who kept my nose to the grindstone with their persistent "Isn't your book finished yet?" Finally, I owe everything to Robert Fleming who, when I had finished a class in Afro-American Literature with him at the University of New Mexico, stopped me in the hall to ask if I had ever read Zora Hurston's *Their Eyes Were Watching God*. At that time, I had never heard of Hurston or her novel. Bob and the novel piqued my interest, and here I am.

LILLIE P. HOWARD

Wright State University

Acknowledgments

I wish to thank the following:

Everette Hurston, executor of the Hurston estate, for permission to quote from all of Zora Neale Hurston's works, including *Seraph on the Suwanee*, Copyright 1948.

The Beinecke, Yale University Library, for permission to quote from material in the James Weldon Johnson Collection.

Howard University Library, for permission to quote from material in the Alain Locke and Arthur Spingarn Collections.

The University of Florida Library, Gainesville, for permission to quote from the Hurston Papers.

Lippincott Publishers for permission to quote from the following:

From the book *Jonah's Gourd Vine* by Zora Neale Hurston. Copyright 1934 by Zora Neale Hurston. Copyright © renewed 1962 by John C. Hurston and Joel Hurston. Reprinted by permission of Lippincott & Crowell, Publishers.

From the book *Mules and Men* by Zora Neale Hurston. Copyright 1935 by Zora Neale Hurston. Copyright © renewed 1963 by John C. Hurston and Joel Hurston. Reprinted by permission of Lippincott and Crowell, Publishers.

From the book *Their Eyes Were Watching God* by Zora Neale Hurston. Copyright 1937 by J. B. Lippincott Company. Copyright © renewed 1965 by John C. Hurston and Joel Hurston. Reprinted by permission of Lippincott & Crowell, Publishers.

From the book *Moses, Man of the Mountain* by Zora Neale Hurston. Copyright 1939 by Zora Neale Hurston. Copyright © renewed 1967 by John C. Hurston and Joel Hurston. Reprinted by permission of Lippincott and Crowell, Publishers.

From the book *Tell My Horse* by Zora Neale Hurston. Copyright 1938 by Zora Neale Hurston. Copyright © renewed 1966 by John C. Hurston and Joel Hurston. Reprinted by permission of Lippincott and Crowell, Publishers.

Chronology

1901(?) Zora Neale Hurston born on January 7 in Eatonville, Florida.

1915 Leaves home to become maid to a member of a traveling Gilbert and Sullivan troupe.

1923– Attends Howard University, Washington, D.C. "John Red-
1924 ding Goes to Sea" published in *Stylus*.

1924 "Drenched in Light" published in December in *Opportunity*.

1925 "Spunk" and *Color Struck* published in June in *Opportunity*.

1926 Wins scholarship to Barnard College. "Muttsy" appears in August in *Opportunity*; "Sweat" appears in *Fire!!*

1927 *The First One* published in James W. Johnson's *Ebony and Topaz*. Marries Herbert Sheen on May 19 in St. Augustine, Florida.

1928 Graduates from Barnard with B.A. degree; comes to the attention of Dr. Franz Boas, noted anthropologist.

1928– Collects folklore in the South.
1931

1931 Divorces Herbert Sheen on July 7.

1933 "The Gilded Six-Bits" published in *Story Magazine*.

1933– Drama instructor at Bethune Cookman College, Daytona,
1934 Florida.

1934 *Jonah's Gourd Vine.*

1935 *Mules and Men.*

1937 *Their Eyes Were Watching God.*

1937– Receives two Guggenheim fellowships to collect folklore
1938 in Jamaica, Haiti, and Bermuda.

1938 *Tell My Horse.*

1938– Works for the WPA in Florida collecting folklore.
1939

1939 *Moses, Man of the Mountain.* Marries Albert Price III on June 27 in Fernandina, Florida.
1941 Becomes staff writer at Paramount Studios in Hollywood.
1942 *Dust Tracks on a Road.*
1943 Divorces Albert Price III on November 9.
1948 *Seraph on the Suwanee.* Arrested on September 13 on a trumped-up morals charge.
1950 Discovered working as a maid in Rivo Alto, Florida.
1956– Librarian at Patrick Air Force Base, Florida.
1957
1958– Reporter for the Fort Pierce, Florida, *Chronicle*; part-time
1959 teacher at Lincoln Park Academy, Fort Pierce.
1960 Dies on January 28 in the County Welfare Home, Fort Pierce, Florida.

CHAPTER 1

Life and Times

ACCORDING to her autobiography, *Dust Tracks on a Road* (1942), Zora Neale Hurston "heard tell" that she was born on January 7, 1903, in Eatonville, Florida, the seventh of eight children. Research has revealed, however, that Zora may have been born as early as 1891—at least one brother says so—but that around hog-killing time in 1901, she was certainly firmly entrenched in Eatonville, Florida, hollering up a storm.[1] She claimed that she was not delivered by the trusty midwife but "just rushed out herself," the umbilical cord being cut by a white man who stopped by a bit later to deliver "a half of a shoat, sweet potatoes, and other garden stuff."[2] She was not the seventh of eight children as she herself "rumored" and perhaps wished— the seventh child was Sunday's child, "bonny," "blithe," "good and gay"—but the sixth, two boys, Everette and Ben, coming after her. She was later to convince Everette to set his age back by seven years so that there would be no obvious discrepancies betweeen what she claimed her age to be at the time and what the correct knowledge of Everette's age would have given the lie to.[3] Her parents were "dark-brown Lucy Ann Potts (1865–1904) of the land-owning Richard Potts" and John Hurston (1861–1917), a wayfaring carpenter, Baptist preacher, mulatto from "over the creek." Lucy and John had met and married in Alabama and had moved to Eatonville, according to Zora, three years before she was born.[4]

Eatonville itself was a rare mecca—a "Negro town," not "the black back-side of an average town," but "a pure Negro town— charter mayor, council, town marshal and all. It was not the first Negro community in America, but it was the first to be incorporated, the first attempt at organized self-government on the part of Negroes in America."[5]

In Eatonville, John Hurston acquired property and quickly

rose to prominence in the community as a carpenter, a Baptist preacher, and finally as moderator of the South Florida Baptist Association. Lucy, a former country schoolteacher, contented herself with domestic chores, sewing for the community and taking care of and teaching a brood of youngsters which augmented almost every year. Though she was the one who urged Zora to "jump at the sun," she remained for the most part in bas relief emerging from the shadows occasionally to take the part of one of her children, often Zora, against the father, and to retrieve the husband from his frequent meanderings. She was a bulwark, thrifty and protective, propping her husband up on every leaning side, advising him about the most productive course to pursue.

Zora and her siblings—Hezekiah Robert, Sarah Emmaline, John Cornelius, Richard William, Clifford Joel, Benjamin, and Everette —grew up in Eatonville with few worries. They lived in an eight-room house and always had plenty to eat—oranges, grapefruit, tangerines, guavas, chickens, eggs, home-cured hog meat, sweet potatoes and other vegetables from their five-acre garden, and, of course, fresh game and fish as often as they could be had.

Zora's childhood—until her mother died on September 19, 1904[6] —seems to have been particularly idyllic, filled with dreams, defiance, make-believe, all the trappings of a happy child. As she "spied noble, grew like a gourd vine, and yelled bass like a gator," she was extremely imaginative and curious, often claiming that the trees, birds, and lake talked to her.

I used to climb to the top of one of the huge chinaberry trees which guarded our front gate and look out over the world. The most interesting thing that I saw was the horizon.... It grew upon me that I ought to walk out to the horizon and see what the end of the world was like. The daring of the thing held me back for a while, but the thing became so urgent that I showed it to my friend, Carrie Roberts, and asked her to go with me. (p. 44)

Carrie Roberts promised but reneged, Zora's father refused to provide the "fine black riding horse with white leather saddle and bridles" which Zora felt necessary for the trip, and so that was that—no horizon. Not to be outdone, however, Zora later set up a similar situation in *Their Eyes Were Watching God* (1937) where the heroine contemplates, explores and achieves the horizon. Through her character, then, Zora's childhood dream becomes a reality. As Robert Bone has noted, Zora's impulse toward wandering and seeking new experiences put her, at an early age, in the picaresque tradition. She, like many of the characters she would later create, was an adventurer, seeking to break "with the fixity of things." As Bone also notes, Zora's impulse toward "far horizon" which informed her movements throughout her life, firmly placed her in the tradition of the Great Migration—the quest for new and better and more exciting experiences, in short, the search for the Promised Land—which preceded the Harlem Renaissance.[7]

When she could snatch time away from the fantasies, Zora attended the local Robert Hungerford school. Having benefited from her mother's teachings, she was an apt pupil who so impressed two Yankee ladies who visited her fifth grade class that they sent her a box of books which included Grimm's fairy tales, Greek and Roman myths, Gulliver's Travels, Dick Whittington, the Norse Tales, Rudyard Kipling's Jungle Books, some Hans Anderson and Robert Louis Stevenson. Zora was already reading the Bible, having chanced upon David—"David went here and he went there, and no matter where he went, he smote 'em hip and thigh"—while idly thumbing through the book as she recovered from a whipping.

I *Twilight Things*

After her mother died in 1904, Zora's father quickly remarried, and to appease his new wife, sent Zora, though underaged, to attend school with a brother and Sarah in Jacksonville. Here Zora was rudely snatched from her fantasy land:

Jacksonville made me know that I was a little colored girl. Things were all about the town to point this out to me. Streetcars and stores and then talk I heard around the school. I was no longer among the white people whose homes I could barge into with a sure sense of welcome. These white people had funny ways. I could tell that even from a distance. . . . School in Jacksonville was one of those twilight things. It was not dark, but it lacked the bold sunlight that I craved.

... I was deprived of the loving pine, the lakes, the wild violets in the woods and the animals I used to know. No more holding down first base on the team with my brothers and their friends. Just a jagged hole where my home used to be.

Because of financial straits and worsening relationships with her father and his wife, Zora was forced to leave school. Her father no longer paid her room and board and even nonchalantly suggested that the school adopt her. When that proved impossible, Zora was returned to the misery of her father's house in Eatonville: "The very walls were gummy with gloom. Too much went on to take the task of telling it. Papa's children were in his way, because they were too much trouble to his wife. Ragged, dirty clothes and hit-and-miss meals. The four older children were definitely gone for good. One by one, we four younger ones were shifted to the homes of Mama's friends."[8]

With few books, sporadic schooling, minimal family love, and no permanent resting place, Zora would "cry inside and be depressed for days until I learned how to mash down on my feelings and numb them for a spell."[9] She "walked by her corpse, smelt it and felt it"; she knew poverty that smelled "like death. Dead dreams dropping off the heart like leaves in a dry season and rotting around the feet; impulses smothered too long in the fetid air of underground caves. The soul lives in a sickly air. People can be slaveships in shoes."[10] Wanting to return to school she knew she would have to find work and pay her way. She was fourteen years old at the time.

She worked periodically as a maid for white people, failing more often than not because she not only refused to act humble but also refused the sexual advances of her male employers. Too, she was more interested in reading than in dusting and dishwashing. She worked for a couple of months as a receptionist in a doctor's office and for several months after that as a kind of live-in maid to her brother Bob and his family. Her first successful job of any duration came when she was hired as a wardrobe girl for a Miss M., a singer in a Gilbert and Sullivan repertory company touring the South. Zora traveled with the group for eighteen months, encountering new experiences, and reading a great deal. The job made her more aware of her rusty spots and provincialism. More than ever she wanted to go to school. When the tour ended, she underwent an appendicitis operation at the free ward of the Maryland General Hospital, and supporting herself with waitress jobs, enrolled in night school in Baltimore; she later registered at Morgan Academy, the high school division of what is now Morgan State University. The Dean of Morgan Academy arranged a live-in job for her with a white clergyman and his wife.

Though Zora studied hard and progressed, at first she felt out of place at school. Her classmates were well-to-do "pretty girls and snappy boys" and there she was with her face "looking like it had been chopped out of a knot of pine wood with a hatchet on somebody's off day"; what was worse, she had "only one dress, a change of underwear and one pair of tan oxfords."[11] When her classmates took little notice of these "drawbacks," however, Zora got along swimmingly, and was often put in charge of her classes.

She spent two years at Morgan Academy finishing in June, 1918. She worked the summer in Washington, D.C., first as a waitress in the exclusive Cosmos Club downtown, then as a manicurist in the 1401 G Street Barber Shop of a Mr. George Robinson, a black man whose G Street shop catered strictly to whites, but who kept a shop uptown for blacks. She entered Howard University in the fall of 1918, attending Howard Prep from 1918–1919 in an effort to ready herself for "the capstone of Negro education."

In 1920, at Howard, she met and fell in love with Herbert Sheen of Decatur, Illinois. Sheen, aspiring to be great, was working his way through Howard as a hotel waiter. Though he later moved to New York, organized a jazz combo—he played piano and sang—toured New Jersey, then entered the University of Chicago and later medical school, Sheen kept his relationship with Zora alive. On May 19, 1927, they married in St. Augustine, Florida. On July 7, 1931, they divorced. Happiness had gone out of the bedroom and taken to living in the parlor after fewer than eight months of the marriage, supposedly because neither spouse could buckle under to the other's career. Zora wanted to pursue her research but felt inhibited by her husband and, as Sheen was later to tell Robert Hemenway, "the demands of her career doomed the marriage to an early, amicable divorce."[12]

While Sheen was taking New Jersey resorts by storm with his jazz combo in 1921, Zora was still at Howard attending stimulating literary discussions at night at the home of the black poet, Georgia Douglas Johnson, and studying by day with Alain Locke, then a young philosophy professor (he produced *The New Negro* only four years later!) at Howard, and head of Stylus, the campus literary club. Having proven her literary talents in her English classes, Zora was admitted to Stylus and, in May 1921, published her first short story, "John Redding Goes to Sea," in *Stylus*, the club's magazine.

II *Opportunity*

"John Redding Goes to Sea" was Zora's calling card on the professional literary world, for because of it, Charles Spurgeon Johnson, who was just founding *Opportunity Magazine*, wrote to her for material. She sent him "Drenched in Light" and later "Spunk" and a play, *Color Struck*. Johnson was introducing new black writers and new material to the public, and on the merit of Zora's works suggested that she come to New York to introduce herself.[13] By that time, Zora was no longer in school, having once again fallen victim to illness and penury. By the first week of January 1925, however, she was in New York City with "$1.50, no job, no friends, and a lot of hope." Immediately befriended by the Johnsons, she managed.

She couldn't have arrived in New York at a more opportune time. The Harlem Renaissance was in vogue and the realization of black dreams seemed imminent. Black writers from all over —Claude McKay from Jamaica, Eric Walrond from Barbados, Langston Hughes from Kansas, Wallace Thurman from Salt Lake City, Jean Toomer and Sterling Brown from Washington, D.C., Rudolph Fisher from Providence, Rhode Island—were flocking to New York to make literary history. Any and everything seemed possible. *Shuffle Along* was playing almost nightly on stage; Duke Ellington and his crowd were holding forth at the famed Cotton Club; Bessie Smith was singing the blues; the charleston and the cakewalk had become decided hits; A'lelia Walker, heiress of Madame C. J. Walker, was giving parties that were so popular that royal personages—a Scandinavian prince in one instance, claims Langston Hughes—were often forced to entertain themselves "in the vicinity" of A'lelia's apartment.[14]

At the first *Opportunity* award dinner, May 1, 1925, Zora won second prize for "Spunk" and met one of the contest's judges, novelist Fannie Hurst. Hurst later hired Zora as a live-in secretary, though, much to her surprise, she soon learned that Zora would be doing more "living-in" than "secretarying." As Hurst remembers it,

she walked into my study one day by telephone appointment, carelessly, a big-boned, good-boned young woman, handsome and light yellow, with no show of desire for the position of secretary for which she was applying. Her dialect was as deep as the deep south, her voice and laughter the kind I used to hear on the levees of St. Louis when I was growing up in that city. As Zora expressed it, we "took a shine" to one another and I engaged her on the spot as my live-in secretary.

What a quaint gesture that proved to be! Her shorthand was short on legibility, her typing hit or miss, mostly the latter, her filing, a game of find-the-thimble. Her mind ran ahead of my thoughts and she would interject with an impatient suggestion or clarification of what I wanted to say. If dictation bored her she would interrupt, stretch wide her arms and yawn: "Let's get out the car, I'll drive you up to the Harlem bad-lands or down to the wharves where men go down to the sea in ships."[15]

Frustrated to her limits, Hurst soon fired Zora as secretary but, no doubt fully aware that she could not find better entertainment anywhere, kept her on as companion and chauffeur.

At the Awards dinner, Zora had also met Annie Nathan Meyer, a novelist and one of the founders of Barnard College, who arranged for a scholarship so that Zora could attend Barnard in the fall. Zora entered Barnard in the fall of 1925 and graduated with a B.A. degree in 1928. Near the end of her studies Zora, who had primarily confined her studies at Barnard to English, political science, history, and geology, was advised to take some fine arts, economics, and anthropology. She started anthropology under Dr. Gladys Reichard who called a term paper of Zora's to the attention of the famed anthropologist Dr. Franz Boas, then teaching at Columbia. Boas took Zora under his wing as an apprentice, and made an anthropologist of her.

Zora took her appenticeship so seriously that when she and
Boas were studying physical characteristics of the race, she often
took a set of calipers and went to Harlem to measure the skulls
of people who passed her on the street. The bravery of this act
is assessed in Langston Hughes's memory of Zora in *The Big Sea*:
"Almost nobody else could stop the average Harlemite on Lenox
Avenue and measure his head with a strange-looking anthropological device and not get bawled out for the attempt, except
Zora, who used to stop anyone whose head looked interesting,
and measure it."[16]

Anthropology gave Zora the analytical tools for returning to
the South and tapping the rich reservoir of material passed
around among black folks every day. Zora knew the material
well and often amused her friends and endeared acquaintances
with racy, side-splitting anecdotes remembered from her Eatonville days and imbibed around Joe Clarke's store porch:

Men sat around the store on boxes and benches and passed this
world and the next one through their mouths. The right and the
wrong, the who, when and why was passed on, and nobody doubted
the conclusions. There were no discreet nuances of life on Joe
Clarke's porch. There was open kindnesses, anger, hate, love, envy
and its kinfolks, but all emotions were naked, and nakedly arrived
at. It was a case of "make it and take it." You got what your strengths
would bring you. This was not just true of Eatonville. This was the
spirit of that whole new part of the state at that time, as it always
is where men settle new lands.[17]

The study of anthropology gave Zora a new perspective on what
she had hitherto only seen as "good old lies" and stories. Robert
Hemenway explains: "When Hurston became fascinated with
anthropology, she acquired the relatively rare opportunity to
confront her culture both emotionally and analytically, both as
subject and as object. She had lived Afro-American folklore
before she knew that such a thing existed as a scientific concept
or had special value as evidence of the adaptive creativity of a
unique subculture. Hurston came to know that her parents and
their neighbors perpetuated a rich oral literature without self-
consciousness, a literature illustrating a creativity seldom recognized and almost universally misunderstood."[18]

Two weeks before she graduated from Barnard, Zora was awarded a $1400 fellowship to collect folklore in the South. The fellowship was arranged by Boas through the Carter Woodson's Association for the Study of Negro Life and History. Boas planned for Zora to spend six months in the field "beginning in Jacksonville and working south through such towns as Palatka and Sanford to Eatonville; if she had time, she would go on to Mobile and New Orleans. The task was to record the songs, customs, tales, superstitutions, lies, jokes, dances, and games of Afro-American folklore."[19]

When she left New York in late February 1927, bound for the South, Zora had high hopes, but Boas was worried that she was a little too much impressed with her own accomplishments. He had good reason to be for Zora failed to make the necessary transition from abstract scientific theory to concrete, very un-scientific people: "When I went about asking, in carefully-ac-cented Barnardese, 'Pardon me, do you know any folk-tales or folk-songs?' the men and women who had whole treasuries of material seeping through their pores looked at me and shook their heads. No, they had never heard of anything like that around there. Maybe it was over in the next county. Why didn't I try over there? I did, and got the self-same answer."[20] The result—empty pages, humility, and misery. "O, I got a few items," she later said in her autobiography. "But compared with what I did later, not enough to make a flea a waltzing jacket. Considering the mood of my going South I went back to New York with my heart beneath my knees and my knees in some lonesome valley. I stood before Papa Franz and cried salty tears."[21]

Later, Zora was able to appease both Boas and the hard taskmaster Woodson with an account of the black settlement established at St. Augustine by the Spaniards in the seventeenth century, and an article, "Cudjo's Own Story of the Last African Slaver," the results of an interview Zora had conducted with Cudjo Lewis of Mobile, Alabama; Lewis was the only survivor of the last-known ship to bring African slaves to America. Unfortunately the article was not really Zora's work, though she did spend some time with Lewis in Mobile in July and December of 1927. As the linguist William Stewart discovered in 1972, how-ever, Zora culled the bulk of the material for her "original" paper

from Emma Langdon Roche's *Historic Sketches of the Old South*
(New York: Knickerbocker Press, 1914).

Zora was able to return to the field to collect more folklore
when she came under the auspices of Mrs. Charlotte Osgood
Mason, a wealthy white Park Avenue woman who supported
Indian Arts, Afro-American Arts, and any other endeavors which
she felt smacked of primitivism. As something of a fairy godmother and often a surrogate parent who also insisted upon
being called "godmother," she variously supported Alain Locke,
Langston Hughes, Miguel Covarrubias, Louise Thompson, Aaron
Douglas, and Richmond Barthé, all of whom she encouraged to
indulge and reveal their "innate primitivism." For a time, most
complied, often simulating a primitivism they did not feel, but
as the role became too unbearable a few like Langston Hughes
and Louise Thompson broke away. As Hughes remembers it:
"She wanted me to be primitive and know and feel the intuitions
of the primitive. But, unfortunately, I did not feel the rhythms
of the primitive surging through me, and so I could not live and
write as though I did. I was only an American Negro—who had
loved the surface of Africa and the rhythms of Africa—but I was
not Africa. I was Chicago and Kansas City and Broadway and
Harlem."[22] Unlike Hughes and Thompson, Hurston was able to
play the primitive for several years.

Zora and Mason formally met in September 1927 when Mason,
who had probably learned of Zora from Alain Locke, invited Zora
to her house. Impressed with Zora and convinced of her abilities
to help to record and preserve Afro-American culture, Mason
offered to subsidize Zora's research trips to the South to collect
folklore. A contract between Mason and Hurston was drawn up,
witnessed, signed, and notarized on December 1, 1927. According
to the contract, Zora was to collect material that Mason was
interested in but was too busy to collect herself: "data relating
to the music, folklore, poetry, hoodoo, conjure, manifestations of
art, and kindred matters existing among the American Negroes."[23]
The contract began on December 1, 1927, and was to expire on
December 1, 1928. Mason agreed to pay Zora $2,400, payable in
equal monthly installments of $200 on or about the first day of
each month. She would also furnish one moving picture camera
and one Ford automobile, though Zora would have to purchase

her own car insurance. Zora was "faithfully to perform her task" and "to return to Mason all of said information, data, transcripts of music, etc., which she shall have obtained." Zora was forbidden "to make known to any other person, except one designated in writing by said data or information."[24] Later Mason was to determine what material Zora might display in her revues or what she might publish in her books.

When the contractual year was up, Mason, though not thoroughly pleased with Zora's output, kept her on, supporting her intermittently, often lending her money but always keeping a strict record of accounts due. The contract with Zora was formally ended in March 1931, though Mason continued to extend her largesse to Hurston until fall 1932.

Mason's subsidy gave Zora an opportunity to rectify the mistake she had made on her first folklore-collecting venture in the South. She journeyed to Magazine Point, Alabama, parts of Florida, including Eatonville, Eau Gallie, and the jook joints of Polk County in and surrounding the living quarters of the Everglades Cypress Lumber Company near Loughman, Florida. Unlike her first research trip South when she chaffed under the rebuking eyes of her potential subjects, this trip was successful. Zora had cast aside her condescending "Barnardese" attitude and become more engaging. In some instances, she not only claimed to be a fugitive from the law but she explained her new Chevrolet coupe by saying that she had paid for it with money earned by bootlegging in the hills. She had become one of her subjects, sharing their joys and their sorrows, urging them on to pass down that rich legacy of material. She held lying contests, got the people to play the dozens, to "specify" and "signify." She was in a folklore heaven, but it was a dangerous heaven which often threatened to claim her, body and soul. Her friendship with Big Sweet, a rough and ready inhabitant of the quarters of the Cypress Lumber Company, however, shielded her from many of the shenanigans of the camp. After an almost fatal incident in which Zora barely escaped being knifed to death by a woman jealous of the men's attention to Zora, Zora wisely moved on to New Orleans. In the teeming lumber camp, she had learned a few things about folklore and work songs: "The words do not count. The subject matter in Negro folk-songs can be anything and go from love to work, to travel, to food, to weather, to fight, to demanding the return of a wig by a woman who has turned unfaithful. The tune is the unity of the thing."[25]

In New Orleans, Zora delved into Hoodoo, bodily and spiritually entering the world of Marie Leveau, the legendary hoodoo queen. She apprenticed herself to a number of local hoodoo doctors, the most notorious being Luke Turner, and learned the routines for making and breaking marriages, for driving off and punishing enemies, for influencing the minds of judges and juries in favor of clients, for killing by remote control, and other routines which Zora preferred not to discuss with "commoners."

Zora's mind was ripe for such undertakings. She had always believed in hoodoo, psychic, and spiritual powers. Eatonville had fostered that belief, as she was later to record in her autobiography. During her relationship with Mason, she claimed that a psychic bond had been established between them which would make each privy to the other's thoughts. Once, when Mason was ill, Zora offered to be of help by preparing food, but she had already "set up an altar" and asked the invisible powers to heal Mason. And, when she learned that Locke was not faring well, she "murmured a word for him to the proper forces."[26]

The New Orleans experience steeped Zora in the voodoo culture, causing her to allow voodoo a major role in her first novel, *Jonah's Gourd Vine.*

III   *Deferred Dreams*

The Hurston-Mason correspondence in the Alain Locke Collection at Howard University is filled with evidence of Zora's attempts to live up to the expectations and terms of her contract with Mason. Though involved in a flurry of activities, she was far from the blooming child Mason expected. And, what was worse, Zora was beginning to doubt her own abilities as a writer. On November 25, 1930, almost three years after Mason had signed her on because of her confidence in Zora's abilities to produce, Zora wrote to Mason: "I am trying to get some bone in my legs so that you can see me standing so that I shall cease to worry you. . . . So watch your sun-burnt child do some scuffling. That is the thing that I have lacked—the urge to push hard and insist on a hearing." In a letter to Mason dated September 25, 1931, Zora proposed opening up a chicken business supplying "an exclusive mouth-to-mouth chicken specialist service" to New Yorkers. Zora swore by her "very fine chicken boullion, chicken salad, chicken a la king, and hot, fried chicken" and was considering going into business because "I firmly belive that I shall succeed as a writer, but the time element is important. I know that you worry about my future. Therefore if I had a paying business—which after all could not take up a great deal of my time, I'd cease to be a problem."[27] She obviously felt that Mason might have made a poor investment in her. In the same letter, she promised that if she didn't succeed with the "story book" (probably *Mules and Men*) or with the play *Spunk* (a dramatized version of folklore material she had collected), or with the novel (*Jonah's Gourd Vine*) she was planning, she would graciously bow out of Mason's life: "I want to remain in your love, but I shall take nothing further from you in a material way. I shall feel that perhaps someone with a greater gift deserves your help more than I. You are most magnificent and I feel justified in accepting from you only if you are fostering ability. If I am convinced that I have nothing the world wants then you are too high for my mediocrity to weigh down."[28]

Feeling that the folklore she had collected could be presented to advantage on the stage, Zora was trying to produce some successful revues. She began by assisting the producer Forbes Randolph who was preparing a revue called *Fast and Furious*, "a colored revue in thirty-seven scenes." Zora wrote three sketches and appeared as a pompom girl in another. The revue opened on September 15, 1931, but because of poor reviews, shut down a week later. Zora next wrote sketches for *Jungle Scandals*. When it, too, folded, Zora turned her attention to "Spunk," exclusive songs and dances from her own collected material, which she presented to Hall Johnson, of *Run Little Chillun* fame, to consider for his Hall Johnson Choir. Johnson returned the material with his sentiment that "The world was not ready for Negro music unless it were highly arranged. The barbaric melodies and harmonies were simply not fit for musical ears."[29]

Disgruntled but not discouraged, Zora recruited her own performers, organized a revue of her best material centered

around a single day in a railroad work camp into a show called
The Great Day, and returned to Johnson. When nothing encouraging happened, Zora decided to put on her own show. Though
she had found adept performers, she had to ask Mason for $250
for costumes, publicity and photography. She had already sold
her car to put up deposit for the theatre and had pawned her
radio for $16 to pay carfares for her group of fifty-two people.
Mason loaned her the money and on January 10, 1932, *The Great
Day* opened at the John Golden Theater. The show was a great
success, receiving good reviews. When it was over, however,
Zora again had to borrow money from Mason, this time to pay
the cast. The show had not generated enough money and Zora
felt "too keenly conscious of how far short I fell of the mark at
which I aimed."[30] On March 29, *The Great Day* was offered at
the School for Social Research; shortly thereafter Zora dis-
banded the group. There was at least one very flattering out-
come from this enterprise: "George Antheil, the French composer, paid me the compliment of saying I would be the most
stolen-from Negro in the world for the next ten years at least.
He said that this sort of thievery is unavoidable. Unpleasant, of
course but at the bottom a tribute to one's originality."[31]

January 6, 1932, found Zora working with the Creative Literature Department of Rollins College at Winter Park, Florida, in
an attempt to produce a concert program of Negro Art. The Department hoped to surpass what Paul Green and others were
doing at the University of North Carolina by placing "special
stress on music and drama, but painting, carving, sculpture—
all forms of art to be encouraged." There was one bitter note,
however, which Zora took in stride. Her concert group was to
sing to the general public on January 27, but blacks were not
invited. In early February, the group would perform at Hungerford, "the Negro school." As far as personal problems went, Zora
was intermittently ill, suffering from intestinal trouble; she had
"little food, no toothpaste, no stockings, needed shoes badly,
no soap."[32] She was still floundering, grasping for recognition
and to find her particular niche in life.

By April 4, 1932, Zora was back in New York, only to hear
Alain Locke, as Mason's emissary, suggest that she change to less
expensive living quarters and/or go South and find work. Later

in a letter to Mason, Zora explained that she had written to two schools for employment and was a bit nonplussed to "understand that both you and Alain feel that I have lost my grip on things."[33] Zora was still having intestinal trouble, needed medical attention but sought none because she lacked the necessary fee. She understandably felt that her health was affecting her performance.

She was ecstatic about the idea of moving South, however; not only would the move improve her health, but it would offer an escape from New York, a much-needed change in atmosphere and a chance for self-support.

By May 8, 1932, Zora was in Eatonville, Florida, writing to Mason that she was extremely happy, that she had finished one short story that had been in her mind for four years, and that she would resume work on the story book the following day, then on to the novel she had wanted to write since 1928. She felt "renewed like the eagle. The clang and clamor of New York drops away like a last year's dream."[34]

The pastoral atmosphere of Eatonville worked its magic on Zora. She once again began to hold her head up and look around her, taking pride in the uniqueness of her ancestry, her culture, her roots. In a May 17, 1932, letter to Mason, she wrote: "Eatonville now has a paved street. Do you know that in more than fifty years of this town's existence that never has a white man's child been born here? My father was a mulatto but he was born in Alabama and moved here while young, following his employer and father who settled in the white community. There is no known case of white-Negro affair around here. No white-Negro prostitution ever."[35] In the tradition of Booker T. Washington, she hoped to found an adult school in Eatonville for Blacks. "Somebody ought to consider the great body of Negroes and leave the special cases alone for awhile. I mean by that, that nothing is done to point out to the lowly a better way of conquering his clods. So I shall teach the cooking of stews, beans, bread, vegetables, simple pastries and sewing and indoor painting and furniture making, etc."[36] One would have thought, of course, that the people of Eatonville would have known how to do most, if not all, of what Zora hoped to teach them. At any rate, the school remained simply an idea, and Zora continued her writing.

IV *Mule Bone*

During all of her journeys into the South, Zora had kept in touch with another of Godmother's children, Langston Hughes, though by this time Hughes had left the familial nest. The two had plans of writing a play together. They had lived near each other in New Jersey and had often shared their enthusiasm about the richness of black folk culture. Hughes saw a possible outlet for this enthusiasm when the Theater Guild's Theresa Helburn, whom he met at a party given by Taylor Gordon in late February or early March, suggested that Hughes write a Negro comedy. According to Hughes, he repeated Helburn's suggestion to Zora when he saw her a few days later and suggested that they collaborate. Zora agreed, "and in a short time we went to work, using as a basis a folk-tale that Miss Hurston had about one man who hit another in the head with a mule bone in a quarrel over a turkey."[37] The two men had shot simultaneously at a wild turkey and each claimed the turkey belonged to him. The attacker, the wielder of the mule bone, was charged with assault and battery and brought to trial in the church. The defendant was found guilty when the minister "grabbed the Bible and read about Samson and the Philistines, saying that if Samson could kill ten thousand Philistines with the jawbone of an ass, a mule bone was much worse—and therefore this man should be run out of town (the town had no jail), which he was."[38]

Using this tale as a skeleton, Hughes was to do the construction, plot, characterization, and guide the dialog. Zora was to put in "the authentic Florida color, give the dialog a true Southern flavor, and insert many excellent turns of phrase and 'wise-cracks' which she had in her mind and among her collections." Hughes suggested some changes and additions to the basic story line: the two hunters should be friends for years, one a guitarist, the other a dancer, who made their living by playing for the white folks who came to Florida from up North for the winter; the two would meet a girl, "a fickle high-brown just come down from New York with a white family as maid" (the girl replaces the turkey as catalyst), and would try to "make" her, thus causing a rift in the longtime friendship; the two fight over the girl in front of the village store, and one hits the other in the head with the mule bone; one boy is a Methodist, the other a Baptist, and at the trial the town splits into two religious camps; the Baptist wins; the Methodist minister, his Bible and the defendant are run out of town; later the two friends try to reconcile but are temporarily set at odds when the girl shows up and tries to get one or the other—either will do—as her lover. Zora endorsed Hughes's suggestions, though she hated to part with the turkey, and suggested that during the final act, the two friends could hold a proposing contest in which each tries to out-propose the other. The girl accepts the winner of the contest and offers to get him a job with her white folks. At the mention of the word *work*, the potential bridegroom reneges and hands the girl over to his partner. The partner doesn't cotton to her kind of work either and they both dance off, leaving the girl alone.

Drafts of the first and third acts and scenes of the second act were finished over a period of three or four weeks. Hughes and Hurston worked by dictating to Louise Thompson who had agreed to serve as their stenographer. After the four weeks were up, Zora returned South for the summer with notes and outlines for the trial scene of Act II. She was to finish a draft of the act while she was away. When she and Hughes met again in November[39] in New York, however, Zora failed to keep appointments, canceled others, claimed she had no copies of the play handy to work on, "said she was terribly busy and terribly nervous and couldn't work anyway; said she thought we ought to put the turkey back in the story and cut down on the girl-interest; finally gave me a copy of what she had done in the South, but demanded it back almost at once before I could make a copy of it for myself; said she had to go back South again almost at once; was not home for the last appointment she gave me—and I have not seen her since."[40]

Zora later accounted for her baffling behavior by explaining that she had become jealous over Hughes's growing friendship with Louise Thompson, was convinced that Louise was "a gold digger" trying to become "the first steno[grapher] to try to collect royalties," and had become genuinely concerned when Hughes had suggested that Louise be paid more than the usual typist's fee and that she be made business manager of any Broadway production of the play.[41] Zora thus, in the interest of Hughes, herself, and the play, began to wreak havoc. She broke off their partnership, claimed that the play was entirely her own and that she had had it copyrighted in her name in October (Hughes found no copyright record to verify this). Zora had actually given the play to Carl Van Vechten, a close friend, to read; Van Vechten had been impressed and had sent the manuscript to Barrett Clark, a reader for the Theatre Guild. Clark, certain that the Guild would reject it, especially in its unfinished form, had taken the liberty to inquire of Rowena Jelliffe if the Gilpin Players might be interested. Zora knew nothing of this and still thought the manuscript was in Van Vechten's hands.

When Mrs. Jelliffe, manager of the Gilpin Players in Cleveland, wanted to produce the play, Hughes, anxious to have Mule Bone produced because it would have been the first Negro folk comedy and would have brought recognition to both him and Zora, sought Zora's permission. Zora authorized production but almost immediately withdrew it and threatened Hughes with Mason who, though Hughes's employment by Mason had ended months before, could still put fear in Hughes's heart. She drove to Cleveland to negotiate herself, tacitly consented one afternoon but stormed in the next morning—after somehow discovering overnight that Louise Thompson had recently been in Cleveland—to say that the whole deal was off. That same morning, February 3, 1931, she sent a telegram to Godmother: "Arrived safely; Have put the person on the run; play stopped; Louise Thompson had been sent for to bolster and case; I smashed them all; Be home by weekend; All my Love—Zora."[42] The play, an admirable comedy that would have done both Hurston and Hughes proud, remained unproduced.[43] It was originally called The Bone of Contention. And indeed it was—all for the sake of a girl—Daisy Blunt in the comedy Mule Bone, Louise Thompson in Hughes and Hurston's tragic personal drama.

On January 22, 1931, Hughes had Mule Bone copyrighted in his and Zora's name. Zora, however, seems to have had the last word. In a March 1931 letter to Arthur Spingarn, she wrote:

This is to deny your assertion that you have seen the original script. You have seen what your client *says* is the original script. You evidently forget that your client had my script out in Cleveland and I see did not hesitate to copy off some "emendations." The whole matter is absolutely without honor from start to finish and this latest evidence of trying to make a case by actual theft, "emendations" as you call them, makes me lose respect for the thin[g] altogether. From the very beginning it has been an attempt to build up a case by inference and construction rather than by fact. But all the liberal construction in the world cannot stand against certain things which I have in my possession.

I think it would be lovely for your client to be a playwright but I'm afraid that I am too tight to make him one at my expense. You have written plays, why not do him one yourself? Or perhaps a nice box of apples and a well chosen corner. But never no play of mine.

Hemenway notes the irony of the whole squabble: "Yet in a sense it [the play] was written by neither Hurston nor Hughes. Much of the language in the play belonged to the race itself, making the argument over its ownership even more ironic."[44]

CHAPTER 2

"The Light":
Books and Things

ALL this chaotic while, 1930–1932, Zora had been readying her field notes for publication. She had submitted the manuscript called *Mules and Men* in various forms to various publishers but none had agreed to publish the material. Temporarily putting her folktale manuscript aside, Zora decided to write "Barracoon," a 117-page story about Cudjo Lewis and the last "Black Cargo." According to the preface, Zora had finished the story by April 17, 1931; but the story went no where. Zora's contract with Mason had been formally severed on March 31, 1931, so it was paramount that Zora succeed quickly.

In the fall, George Antheil, the French composer, now acting as amanuensis of Nancy Cunard, contacted Zora to see if she had any folklore essays that Cunard might use in her anthology, *Negro*. Zora happily gave him six essays: "Characteristics of Negro Expression," "Conversions and Visions," "The Sermon," "Mother Catherine," "Uncle Monday," and "Spirituals and Neo-Spirituals." All six were subsequently published in *Negro: An Anthology*—1931–1933, and some are included in contemporary anthologies.

But the story book was the thing and it did not find a publisher until after Zora's first novel, *Jonah's Gourd Vine*, had been accepted for publication by Lippincott. Bertram Lippincott, the editor, had read Zora's "The Gilded Six-Bits" before it appeared in the August 1933 issue of *Story Magazine* and had inquired if she were also working on a novel. Though Zora had not penned a word, she replied that a novel was in the making, wrote one, had it typed on credit, and borrowed the money to cover mailing expenses; the novel was accepted and Zora was on her way to fame.

Lippincott felt good about *Jonah* and wrote to Carl Van Vechten on February 1, 1934, that he felt the book "a really important contribution to the literature on the American Negro."[1] The novel did well and was even recommended by the Book-of-the-Month Club for May.

After showing Lippincott the manuscript for *Mules and Men*, Zora wrote to Van Vechten that she thought Bertram Lippincott liked *Mules* better than *Jonah*, but that he thought it was too short. He wanted 180 pages more than the 65,000 words Zora turned in. He wanted a "$3.50 book."[2] Zora revised and made the book worth $3.50 by condensing an earlier hoodoo article that she had written in 1931 for the *Journal of American Folklore*; this condensed material formed the last third of the book. Franz Boas agreed to endorse the book by writing the preface. *Mules and Men* was published in 1935.

Though *Mules and Men* came first, it took *Jonah's Gourd Vine* to get it published. When Bertram Lippincott, impressed by "The Gilded Six Bits," wondered if Zora were working on a novel, Zora replied in the affirmative and "the very next week I moved up to Sanford where I was not so much at home as at Eatonville and could concentrate more and sat down to write *Jonah's Gourd Vine*." She claimed that the idea for the novel had come to her in 1929 while she was collecting folklore but "the idea of attempting a book seemed so big, that I gazed at it in the quiet of the night, but hid it away from even myself in daylight."[3] Too, she was laboring under the expectations and prescriptions black writers were supposed to live up to and follow. She wanted to tell a story about "a man" while "Negroes were supposed to write about the Race Problem." Because black writers were "supposed" to say certain things, Zora decided that what was being written and declaimed "was a pose. A Negro writer or speaker was supposed to say those things. It has such a definite pattern as to become approximately folklore."[4] As Alice Walker was to assert years later, "Black writing has suffered, because even black critics have assumed that a book that deals with the relationships between members of a black family—or between a man and a woman—is less important than one that has white people as a primary antagonist. The consequence of this is that many of our books by "major" writers (always male), tell us little about the culture, history, or future, imagination, fantasies, etc., of black people, and a lot about isolated (often improbable) or limited encounters with a nonspecific white world."[5]

Zora began writing *Jonah* on July 1, 1933, finished on September 6, had the manuscript typed on credit, borrowed two dollars for mailing expenses from the treasurer of the local Daughters of the Elks and sent the manuscript to Lippincott on October 3. The book was accepted by October 16 and was published the first week of May 1934.

The reviews were positive, praising the novel's rich language but obviously ignoring the quintessence of the book. Zora was particularly irked by the *New York Times* assessment that the preacher's sermon in the novel "is too good, too brilliantly splashed with poetic imagery to be the product of any one Negro preacher." After reading that disclaimer Zora wrote to a fellow native Floridian, James Weldon Johnson, who understood and could verify the authenticity of the preacher and the sermon:

I suppose that you have seen the criticism of my book in The New York Times. He means well, I guess, but I never saw such a lack of information about us. It just seems that he is unwilling to believe that a Negro preacher could have so much poetry in him. When you and I (who seem to be the only ones even among Negroes who recognize the barbaric poetry in their sermons) know that there are hundreds of preachers who are equalling that sermon weekly. He does not know that merely being a good man is not enough to hold a Negro preacher in an important charge. He must also be an artist. He must be both a poet and an actor of a very high order, and then he must have the voice and figure. He does not realize or is unwilling to admit that the light that shone from GOD's TROMBONES was handed to you, as was the sermon to me in *Jonah's Gourd Vine*.

I wish that you would write an article about Negro preachers that would explain their hold upon their people truthfully. That is, because they are the first artists, the ones intelligible to the masses. Like Adam Bede, a voice has told them to sing of the beginning of things."[6]

Between 1933 when Lippincott noticed "The Gilded Six Bits"

and the publication of her second novel in 1937, Zora spent some time presenting *From Sun to Sun* to audiences in the Florida area. The success of these concerts brought her to the attention of Mary McLeod Bethune, president of Bethune-Cookman College in Daytona Beach. In December 1933 Mrs. Bethune invited Zora to establish a school of dramatic arts at the college. Gratified, Zora went but was soon put off by the iron will of Mrs. Bethune and her expectation that Zora would perform miracles. Though Zora was able to pull off a successful performance of *From Sun to Sun*, casting several members of the student body, by May, 1934, she had decided to "abandon the farce of Bethune-Cookman's Drama Department and get on with my work."[7]

Zora next took some of her performers to the April 29–May 2 National Folk Festival in St. Louis. She wrote to Van Vechten that, though the venture would not pay any money, "it will increase my standing as a Negro folklorist outside of calling attention to me generally."[8] By fall, Zora had been contacted by a Chicago group interested in another *Great Day* concert. On her way to Chicago, Zora gave a small concert at Fisk University in Nashville. The president of the college was so impressed that he encouraged Zora to apply for a teaching position there. When she did, the president, for reasons unknown, kindly rejected her application.

In Chicago, Zora called her new show *Singing Steel*, found performers in local YWCA classes and presented the show on November 23 and 24, 1934. As happenstance would have it, officials of the Julius Rosenwald Foundation were among *Singing Steel*'s audience. Recognizing talent and promise when they saw it, they invited Zora to apply for a fellowship to study for a Ph.D. in anthropology and folklore at Columbia University. The foundation offered her $3,000 for two years of study which would hopefully terminate with the doctorate degree. When they found Hurston's degree plan unacceptable, however, they reduced the fellowship to $700 and decreed that it would only cover the period from December 1, 1934, to June 30, 1935. If they were satisfied with her progress, they would consider renewing the fellowship.

Zora objected to the rigorous, partly "irrelevant" schedule that had been worked out with Boas at Columbia, assured

Rosenwald that she was enrolled and found their terms satis-
factory and then took off for more congenial parts, awarding
interviews to various newspapers, dropping delicious tidbits
about *Jonah's Gourd Vine* and the forthcoming *Mules and Men*,
and sitting in the seat of honor at a tea given by Annie Nathan
Meyer, who had been responsible for Zora's fellowship to
Barnard. (The less honorable seats were filled by Fannie Hurst,
Pearl Buck, Bertram Lippincott, Robert Nathan, Sir Gerald and
Lady Campbell.) Zora also signed on with Alan Lomax and Mary
Elizabeth Barnicle who were embarking on a collection expedi-
tion for the Music Division of the Library of Congress.

And somehow, miraculously through it all, Zora had found
time to entangle herself in a love affair which didn't work out.
No names were given but she did write to Carl Van Vechten
thanking him for befriending her "in such a noble manner, in
the hour of my dumb agony" and explaining to him that in
addition to her perpetual financial problems, "a love affair was
going wrong too at the time. I think it is o.k. now. You know
about it already." Her "agony" had been so great—partly because
of money woes, partly because of the aborted love affair—that
she had gone to the country "guest of the James Huberts of the
Urban League" to recover. "That restored my sanity I believe.
Honest, Carlo, I had got to the place I was talking to myself."[9]

In the fall of 1935, Zora joined the WPA Federal Theater
Project. She needed a job but the Project was ideal for she had
been trying to dramatize and call attention to the black folk
experience. Zora wrote *The Fiery Chariot*, a one-act play, during
this time to be included in the Rollins College performance of
From Sun to Sun. The play, a comedy, was certain to generate
laughter. Set on a southern plantation "before surrender," the
play cast Ike, a tall black, religious man who prays nightly for
God to "come in a good time and git yo humble servant and
keer im to heben wid you" to relieve him of "dis sin-sick world
where Massa work me so-ooo hard and Ah ain't got no rest
nowhere"; the white massa who, grown weary of Ike's loud
exhortations, decides to don a white sheet, play God, and deliver
Ike from his miseries; Ike's wife, Finah, who takes all in stride,
including the "Lawd's" coming to claim Ike; and a son who
wonders about the fate of his father now that "the Lawd" has

finally arrived. When the disguised Massa states his godly mission, Ike, incredulous, stalls for time and finally runs away, daring the Lawd to catch him. When the son asks his mother what his father's chances are of being caught, Finah replies, "You know God ain't got no time wid you' pappy and him barefooted too." The play was never staged and is now among the Hurston papers at the University of Florida, Gainesville.

While working with the WPA Federal Theater Project, Zora became the recipient of a Guggenheim Fellowship to collect folklore in the West Indies. She accepted the Guggenheim on March 18, 1936, resigned her WPA job on March 20, and by April 14 she was in the Caribbean, collecting material which was to be included in her second book of folklore, *Tell My Horse* (1938). She stopped at Haiti and Kingston, Jamaica, proposing to make an exhaustive study of Obeah (magic) practices to add to and compare with what she had already collected in the United States.[10]

When she returned to Haiti after extensive work in Jamaica, the romantic atmosphere triggered what had been "dammed up in" her since she had left the United States, determined to give no more thought to a twenty-three-year-old college student who had put her in this pickle. The student had been a member of the cast for *The Great Day* and was studying to be a minister. He and Zora became enchanted with each other but true to character, Zora took to the road leaving the young man in doubt about the extent or sincerity of her feelings. She released her intense emotions on paper, writing in seven weeks, "under internal pressure," what was to become her best novel, *Their Eyes Were Watching God* (1937). She sent the completed manuscript to Lippincott, and having therapeutically spewed out the agony and achieved much-needed catharsis, returned calmly to the material for *Tell My Horse*. *Their Eyes Were Watching God* was published on September 18, 1937.

When she discovered that she needed more time and money for her project, Zora wrote to Guggenheim on January 6, 1937, requesting a renewal of her fellowship. The renewal was granted in late March and Zora plunged even deeper into her work and the folkways of her subjects. She became violently ill at one point—"For a whole day and a night, I'd thought I'd never make it"—attributing her sufferings to her undue pryings into the rituals of the Petro gods who were "terrible, wicked, powerful and quick." The Petro gods were clearly retaliating, putting the "foreign upstart" into her place. After an unexpected recovery, Zora understandably balked at the idea of continued research abroad and headed for the safety of home. By late September, she was stateside, trying to decide whether to write two books— one that would be safe and acceptable, and another "for the way I want to write it."[11]

She touched base with her publishers in New York but went on to Florida in February to write when Lippincott became impatient for the *Tell My Horse* manuscript. She finished in mid-March and the book was scheduled for publication in October. The book did not sell well, partly because Zora, no political analyst, tried to analyze the politics of the West Indies, and partly because the book was less interesting than *Mules and Men*. Harold Courlander of the *Saturday Review* called it "a curious mixture of remembrance, travelogue, sensationalism and anthropology. The remembrances are vivid, the travelogue tedious, the sensationalism reminiscent of Seabrook and the anthropology a melange of misinterpretation and exceedingly good folklore."[12] How ironic. Zora had almost given up her life for the book.

While awaiting the publication of *Tell My Horse*, Zora joined the Florida Federal Writers Project, and on April 25, 1938, became the editor of the Florida volume of the American Guide series. As an editor who was more "out" than "in," Zora gained a reputation as "an actress who loved to show off, a woman of remarkable talent and spirit, a loner, an uncooperative co-worker, an editor who hated to stay inside at her desk."[13]

In spite of her reputation as a somewhat flighty person, Zora was instrumental in helping to compile *The Florida Negro* which aimed to chronicle "the true history and present status of the black American experience."[14] The volume was completed but never published.

Zora's next job, beginning in fall 1939, was with the North Carolina College for Negroes at Durham where she was hired to organize a drama program. During her year at Durham, she never produced a single play, pleading lack of support from the college administration, and lack of a proper frame for working (no courses in play writing, direction, and production) as her excuse. Actually, Zora was spending much of her time with Paul Green of the drama department at Chapel Hill, "starring" in his Sunday evening play-writing seminar which met at Green's home. Zora had met Green when she spoke at the October meeting of the Carolina Dramatic Association. Like other members of the audience, Green had been impressed by the speech and had invited Zora to his Sunday evening sessions. She and Green became excited about the prospect of doing a play—*John de Conqueror*—together, and Zora may have begun to see her teaching duties at Durham as something of a burden. On January 24, 1940, she wrote to Green (Green has letter in his possession): "You do not need to concern yourself with the situation here at the school. I won't care what happens here or if nothing happens here so long as I can do the bigger thing with you. My mind is hitting on sixteen cylinders on the play now. . . . I see no reason why the firm of Green and Hurston should not take charge of the Negro playrighting [*sic*] business in America, and I can see many reasons why we should."[15]

Zora may not have been doing much teaching at North Carolina College and she was certainly creating no drama department, but it soon became apparent that she had nonetheless been hard at work. In November 1939 her third novel, *Moses, Man of the Mountain*, was published by Lippincott. Readers have been hard put to determine the value of the book, even Robert Hemenway calling it a masterpiece at one point and a noble failure at another.[16] Darwin Turner concluded, "If she had written nothing else Miss Hurston would deserve recognition for this book,"[17] but Alain Locke and Ralph Ellison disagreed, the one calling the novel "caricature instead of portraiture,"[18] the other claiming that "for Negro fiction, it did nothing."[19] Zora herself had been disappointed with her efforts, writing to Carl Van Vechten on October 12, 1939, that "I fell far short of my ideal in the writing."[20] Lippincott, on the other hand, had been hopeful and on October 4, 1939, had written to Van Vechten thanking him for recommending the book and adding: "It confirms our opinion that this is a remarkable book, possibly a great book."[21] The "remarkability" and possibility of greatness of the book remain in question.

In addition to her misgivings about *Moses, Man of the Mountain,* Zora had other problems. She had snuck away during the summer and become entangled with yet another young man, this one at least fifteen years her junior—Albert Price III. On June 27, 1939, she had married Price in Fernandina, Florida. As Hemenway's research has revealed, Zora and Albert had met when they were both involved with the WPA Projects, Price as a WPA Playground Worker. Zora sued for divorce in February 1940, itemizing Price's shortcomings. Price countersued, claiming, among other things, that he was "put in fear of his life due to the professed practice on the part of the Plaintiff in what is termed as 'Black Magic' or 'Voodooism,' claimed by the Plaintiff to have been acquired by her while living in Haiti and that she had the power both in spirits and in the uses of certain preparations to place individuals under certain spells and that if the Defendant would not perform her wishes she possessed the power to 'FIX HIM.' "[22]

The divorce was not finalized until November 9, 1943, because the two principals temporarily reconciled. While Zora was off at North Carolina teaching and representing herself as a single woman, then, Price was back in Florida, probably being very curious about the whereabouts of his bride.

In the winter of 1940–41, Zora was in New York, contemplating what to write next. Her publisher suggested an autobiography, explaining that it could be the first volume of a multivolume work. After writing the book, Zora wrote to a friend, Hamilton Holt, that she "did not want to write it at all, because it is too hard to reveal one's inner self, and still there is no use in writing that kind of book unless you do."[23]

Zora did write it, however, in style in California, having been invited there to live with a rich friend, Katharine Mershon. She made the move in late spring 1941. By mid-July she had completed the first draft but was forced to delete and rewrite because of the Japanese attack on Pearl Harbor. Zora had been hard on America in her first draft, but when the air was filled with patriotism, she thought it expedient to omit the part about American marines who considered "machine gun bullets good laxatives for heathens who get constipated with toxic ideas about a country of their own;" and the part about democracy—

"As I see it, the doctrines of democracy deal with the aspirations of men's souls, but the application deals with things. One hand in somebody else's pocket and one on your gun and you are highly civilized. Your heart is where it belongs—in your pocket book. Put it in your bosom and you are backward. Desire enough for your own use and you are a heathen."[24] There were a few other "choice morsels," some of which she left in, prompting a Lippincott editor to write across the bottom of her manuscript, "Suggest eliminating international opinions as irrelevant to autobiography."[25]

While Zora revised, she worked as a story consultant at Paramount Studios from October 1941 to January 1942 and then lectured at various black colleges. By the summer of 1942, she was back in Florida putting finishing touches on her book, writing plays, and collecting some folklore. The autobiography, *Dust Tracks on a Road*, was published in late November 1942.

Unlike *Moses, Man of the Mountain*, *Dust Tracks on a Road* was extremely succesful, not only selling well but also winning the Anisfield-Wolf Award for "the best book on race relations and for the best volume in the general field of fiction, poetry, or biography which is of such a character that it will aid in the sympathetic understanding and constructive treatment of race relations." There were detractors, however, with Arna Bontemps concluding that "Miss Hurston deals very simply with the more serious aspects of Negro life in America—she ignores them. She has done right well by herself in the kind of world she found."[26] Harold Preece denounced the book as "the tragedy of a gifted, sensitive mind, eaten up by an egocentrism fed on the patronizing admiration of the dominant white world."[27]

Zora had obviously said in *Dust Tracks on a Road* what the "dominant white world" wanted to hear. She was swamped by requests for magazine articles. She published several in *American Mercury*, *Saturday Evening Post*, *Negro Digest*, and *Reader's Digest* between 1942 and 1945. She was lauded by the white world, but suspiciously regarded and often lampooned by the black. After reading some outrageous Hurston comments in a *World Telegram* article (February 1, 1943) in which Zora claimed that "the Jim Crow system works," Roy Wilkins was prompted to write that Zora had gone too far: "Now is no time for tongue-wagging by Negroes for the sake of publicity. The race is fighting a battle that may determine its status for fifty years. Those who are not for us, are against us."[28] In a December 1945 *Negro Digest* article, "Crazy for This Democracy," however, Zora wrote that she was "all for the repeal of every Jim Crow law in the nation here and now. Not in another generation or so. The Hurstons have already been waiting for eighty years for that. I want it here and now. . . . I give my hand, my heart and head to the total struggle. I am for complete repeal of all Jim Crow laws in the U.S. once and for all, and right now. For the benefit of this nation and as a precedent to the world. . . . Not in some future generation, but repeal *now* and forever."[29] In spite of the fervent sincerity of this piece, Zora was never able to live down her reputation in the black community. Eight years later, Lester B. Granger of the *California Eagle* was to respond to Zora's "A Negro Voter Sizes Up Taft" with: "Miss Hurston has written only seldom in recent years and so far as her Negro public is concerned, when she has come out with a production it has been readily evident that she 'shoulda stood in bed.' " He called Zora's article "cheesy" and said that it "smelled to high heaven."[30]

When World War II began, Zora was living in Saint Augustine, writing and teaching part-time at Florida Normal, the local black college. She became incensed by injustices levied against black servicemen in training at the school, and in November 1942 she wrote to Walter White, executive secretary of the NAACP, to vent her wrath. "Dear Walter White," she began. "Well, the Negroes have been bitched again! I mean this Signal Corps school which the government has set up here. It would be more than worth your while to look into the matter. It is awful, Walter. The government, having been forced by you to grant this Signal Corp to Negroes, dumped it in this little hole, and felt that your mouth was stopped. Remember that this is the ONLY one for Negroes in the U.S., though the whites have several. I feel that the whole body of Negroes are being insulted and mocked. Please send someone to look into things. . . . I am only giving you a *hint*. There is plenty here to find out. It concerns us all, and I really think something ought to be done."[31]

Before the dispute at Florida Normal was settled, Zora moved to Daytona Beach where she purchased *Wanago*, a houseboat she later described to Marjorie Kinnan Rawlings, a St. Augustine novelist whom she'd befriended, as thirty-two feet long with a forty-four horsepower Gray motor and sufficient sleeping space. Zora's permanent berth was at the Howard Boat Works in Daytona Beach but she traveled up and down the Halifax and Indian rivers taking in the breathless scenery, enjoying life.

In March she journeyed to Washington, D.C., to receive Howard University's distinguished alumni award, but, from 1942–1944, *Wanago* was her home. She was happy, confident in herself and in her abilities, so much so that she could write to Marjorie Rawlings offering effusive praise for *Cross Creek*, calling Rawlings sister because Rawlings looked at plants and animals and people the way Hurston did and offered authentic presentation of black characters.[32]

Things were going so well for Zora that there was a proposed marriage to James Howell Pitts, a Cleveland businessman with a pharmacy degree from Meharry Medical College. The marriage was expected to occur sometime in January of the following year. Though the marriage announcement appeared on February 5, 1944, in the *New York Amsterdam News*, there is no mention of it in Zora's letters to her friends. She was indeed a woman who kept her private affairs private. As far as is known, however, the marriage never took place.

The spring of 1944 found Zora in New York working with a white woman, Dorothy Waring, on the script for the musical comedy "Polk County." The script was to combine material from *Mules and Men, Mule Bone*, and "High John de Conqueror." The play was copyrighted in 1944 as "Polk County," a Comedy of Negro Life on a Sawmill Camp with authentic Negro Music in three acts, by Zora N. Hurston and Dorothy Waring. On July 31, 1944, the following announcement appeared in the *New York Daily News*: "Stephen Kelen-d'Oxylion has acquired the rights to "Polk County," a comedy of Negro life by Neale Hurston and Dorothy Waring, and is scheduling it for fall publication." Finding it expedient to set up residence in New York until she learned the fate of "Polk County," Zora returned to Florida for her houseboat. By November she had berthed *Wanago* in Manhattan and settled back to await encouraging news of the musical. The

news was long in coming and during the interim, Zora got the
opportunity to challenge the reputation she had acquired in the
black community. Interviewed by a reporter for the *New York
Amsterdam News*, Zora said: "A writer's material is controlled
by publishers who think of the Negro as picturesque. . . . There
is an over-simplication of the Negro. He is either pictured by
the conservatives as happy, picking his banjo, or by the so-called
liberals as low, miserable, and crying. The Negro's life is neither
of these. Rather, it is in-between and above and below these
pictures. That's what I intend to put in my new book."[33]

I   *Far Horizons*

By fall, Zora was restless and considered a trip to Honduras,
Central America, where she hoped to discover an ancient Mayan
City. Told of the city in the fall of 1944 by Reginald Brett, an
English gold miner in British Honduras, Zora found the prospect
irresistible and immediately wrote to the Guggenheim Foundation for subsidy. When the funding wasn't readily forthcoming—
the Guggenheim people were less enthusiastic than she—Zora
settled down to write a novel. On July 15, 1945, she wrote to
Carl Van Vechten that she had been so ill that she had expected
to die and hadn't written to trouble anyone with her miseries
because she wanted to take her leave in silence. She invited
Van Vechten and his wife to accompany her to Honduras where
she hoped to gather material for a book she was planning. She
wanted Van Vechten to illustrate the book. Zora planned to
take the trip aboard the *Maridome*, a schooner owned by a Miami
adventurer, Capt. Fred Irvine. She described Irvine as an Englishman friend of hers, "an adventurous soul like me who wants
to go along for the pure hell of the thing. . . . He is a good
navigator, full of humor, and has your own trait of sincerity in
things. Straight and frank, even at the risk of being unpleasant
for the moment, but a staunch and loyal friend. . . . Thirty-one
years old, handsome, virile, and daring as hell."[34]

Her next letter to Van Vechten, September 12, 1945, came from
aboard her new boat, the *Sun Tan*, in Daytona Beach. She explained that she had done a book for Lippincott but had not received the editorial suggestions for changes which she wanted to

finish before she embarked for Honduras. She also mentioned
another novel she had wanted to write, a serious novel, *Mrs.
Doctor*, on the upper strata of Negro life. She had it two-thirds
done when Lippincott "(timid soul) decided that the American
public was not ready for it yet." So she had done a book on
her native village, starting with the material of *Mule Bone* and
writing a story about a village youth, expelled from town by
village politics, going places, including Heaven and Hell, and returning to the town after seven years to achieve his childhood
ambition of being a fireman on the railroad and the town hero.[35]
Because it failed to live up to the standards of Hurston's other
works, the novel was rejected by Lippincott.

Perhaps Zora had been so sloppy in her writing of the novel
because she was "burning to write" another story, one about
"the 3000 years struggle of the Jewish Peoples for democracy
and the rights of man." The last four and one-half pages of the
September 12 letter to Van Vechten burned with Zora's fervor
for the story of the Jews. She felt that Christians read the Bible
with their own prejudices and not with their eyes. Her proposed title for the book was *Under Fire and Cloud*. She planned
to write the entire book in longhand because she felt it was
"going to be a really great book."

Since her book had been rejected by Lippincott, there were
no revisions to be done, so Zora again contemplated her Honduras
trip. In her July 15 letter to Van Vechten, she claimed that she
had enough money to make the trip to Central America (she
didn't divulge the source of the money), but between July and
September she must have spent much of it, for she was again
short of funds. To supply the lack, she took a job in New York
in the Harlem congressional campaign of Grant Reynolds, who
was opposing Adam Clayton Powell. The *Pittsburgh Courier*
(September 28, 1946) carried a "Harlem Portrait" of Zora men-
tioning her interests in the problems of juvenile delinquency and
her involvement in the famous "block mothers" plan. She told the
interviewer: "It's an old idea, trite but true, of helping people
to help themselves that will be the only salvation of the Negro in
this country."[36] In spite of Zora's unflagging help, Reynolds was
defeated in November 1946; Zora was again out of work and the
trip to Honduras was as far away as ever.

Her friendship with Marjorie Rawlings paid off, however, and Rawlings's publisher, Scribner's, took an interest in Zora's work. By May 1947 Zora had switched publishers, sold Maxwell Perkins, the editor at Scribner's, the option on a new novel, later called *Seraph on the Suwanee* (1948), and taken off for Honduras. She settled at Puerto Cortes, taking quarters in the Hotel Cosenza. Her commitment with Scribner's meant that at first much of her time would be taken up with writing, but she would be able to snatch a few moments for some anthropological adventures. She began to feel comfortable with herself. While in New York, she later confided to Van Vechten, she had kept pretty much to herself because "people were telling brazen lies and the place was too much of a basement to Hell to suit me. . . . I am afraid that I got a little unbalanced. I got so that it was torture for me to go to meet people, fearing the impact of all the national, class and race hate that I would have to listen to. I am praying that my country will have returned to sanity before I get home again."[37]

When her money ran out, she requested another advance from Scribner's, got it, and continued to write. Maxwell Perkins died while Zora was in Honduras, and was replaced by Burroughs Mitchell. Zora finished the novel by September 1947 and mailed it to New York. Before the novel became *Seraph on the Suwanee*, it was variously called *Angel in the Bed, Sang the Suwanee in the Spring, The Seraph's Man, Good Morning Sun, Sign of the Sun*, Zora being unable to make up her mind about the title. By February 1948 she had revised the novel, and Scribner's had accepted it and requested her presence in New York for final editorial decisions. Zora left Honduras on February 20; by March 17 the novel had been scheduled for fall publication. It appeared on October 11, 1948, as *Seraph on the Suwanee*.

Zora's readers were in for a surprise. Lo and behold, the woman who had been steeped in, and who had explored the multifariousness of blackness, had written a novel about white people.

Though the reviews for *Seraph* were, for the most part, favorable, Zora admitted to Marjorie Rawlings that "I am not so sure that I have done my best, but I tried. I need not tell you that my goal still eludes me. I am in despair because it keeps ever ahead of me."[38] At a time when Zora should have been realizing the fruits of her labor, she was more distraught, dissatisfied, and uncertain than ever. The worst, however, was yet to come.

II *Twilight Again*

On September 13, 1948, Zora, living at 140 W. 112th Street, was arrested by New York police and charged with committing an immoral act with a ten-year-old boy. According to the *New York Age*, charges against Zora were brought by Alexander Miller of the Children's Society, who claimed that Zora had committed sodomy with three under-teenage school boys. Specific charges were made by Hurston's ex-landlady, the mother of the ten-year-old, who related incidents she claimed had occurred while Zora was a roomer at her residence at W. 124th Street. The boy's testimony was admitted as evidence. Zora entered a plea of not guilty, offering as proof her passport, showing that she had been in Honduras at the time of the alleged crime. She even offered to take a lie-detector test, but her offer went unnoticed; the charges remained. The boy claimed that his relationship with Zora lasted over a year, beginning sometime during 1946–47, when Zora was in New York and keeping much to herself for reasons she explained in the July 30, 1947, letter to Van Vechten. Though she had been in New York the first part of the period, she was in Honduras during most of the time the boy claimed she was meeting him each Saturday afternoon at a coal bin. The boy mentioned one specific meeting on August 15, 1948, when, unfortunately for him, Zora was in Rhinebeck, New York, gathering material for a magazine article about Constance Seabrook.

When Zora's lawyer, Lewis Waldman, presented all his evidence to the district attorney, Frank Hogan, Hogan decided to conduct a full-scale investigation. He found the child to be mentally disturbed and that Zora had not only told the mother as much two years before but had also suggested that the mother take the child to Bellevue for psychiatric testing. On the basis of this evidence, Hogan decided to drop all charges.

His decision came too late. An employee of the courts had already leaked the story to black newspapers. The headlines in the *New York Age* read: "Noted Novelist Denies She 'Abused'

10-Year-Old Boy: Zora Hurston Released on Bail." The *Afro-American* of Baltimore, Maryland, was even more horrid. Not only was its caption, "Boys, 10, Accuse Zora," on the front page, but the paper also featured a two-column story—"Novelist Arrested on Morals Charge. Reviewer of Author's Latest Book Notes Character Is 'Hungry for Love.'" The story alluded to Worth T. Hedden's review of *Seraph* which had appeared in the *New York Herald Tribune Book Review* on October 10, 1948. Hedden had quoted Jim Meserve's admission to his wife in *Seraph* that, while she loved like a coward, he "was hungry as a dog for a knowing and a doing love." The *Afro-American* article implied that Zora had known the same hunger and had satiated it with the ten-year-old boy in question. Zora was so devastated that on October 30 she wrote to Carl Van Vechten: "The thing is too fantastic, too evil, too far from reality for me to conceive of it. ...One inconceivable horror after another swept over me. I went out of myself, I am sure, though no one seemed to notice. It seemed that every hour some other terror assailed me, the last being the Afro-American sluice of filth." She felt particularly betrayed by her people and her country:

I care nothing for anything anymore. My country has failed me utterly. My race has seen fit to destroy me without reason, and with the vilest tools conceived of by man so far. A society, eminently Christian, and supposedly devoted to super-democracy has gone so far from its announced purpose, not to *protect* children, but to exploit the gruesome fancies of a pathological case and do this thing to human decency. Please do not forget that this thing was not done in the South, but in the so-called liberal North. Where shall I look in the country for justice?

This has happened to me, who has always believed in the essential and eventual rightness of my country. I have been on my own since I was fourteen, scuffling my way through high school and college, and as you know, I have never lived an easy life, but struggled on and on to achieve my ideals. I have believed in America; I have fought the good fight; I have kept the faith. ...

All that I have ever tried to do has proved useless. All that I have believed in has failed me. I have resolved to die. It will take a few days for me to set my affairs in order, and then I will go...no acquittal will persuade some people that I am innocent. I feel hurled down a filthy privy hole.[39]

Zora did not die, but instead pulled herself up by her bootstraps and continued with her life and her writing. She published articles in national magazines and sold an option on her next novel to Scribner's. Her old friend Fred Irvine offered adventure and escape to friendlier climes. Zora joined him in Florida, but the proposed trip out of the country never materialized. As usual, money was the problem.

In March 1950 Zora was found working as a maid in Rivo Alto, Florida. The story broke when Zora's employer, a white woman, discovered one of her stories, "Conscience of the Court," in the *Saturday Evening Post*. The *Miami Herald* learned of the incident and sent a reporter to investigate. In what amounted to an apologia for not writing, Zora told the reporter that "you can use your mind only so long, then you have to use your hands. It's just the natural thing. I was born with a skillet in my hands. Why shouldn't I do it for someone else a while? A writer has to stop writing every now and then and live a little. You know what I mean?" The reporter concluded that "Miss Hurston believes that she is temporarily written out," but had he been following Zora's career, he would have been suspicious of the reasons she gave him. After all, Zora had used her hands all of her life. Even while she was publishing avidly she entertained friends with her "hand chicken (fried chicken to be eaten with the hands)"; and as stated earlier, she even considered opening a chicken joint in which she would fry enough chicken to supply all the chicken lovers in New York. She was constantly offering to fix her "famous" soup for Mason and Alain Locke when they were feeling "puny," and so "the natural thing" during that period of her life, and indeed throughout her life, seemed to have been to use mind and hands simultaneously.

Zora had told the reporter that three short stories and her eighth book were in the hands of her agent; that's as far as they got. Most of her fictional works during this period were unpublishable; her talent seems to have taken up residence elsewhere. She became preoccupied with unusual subjects. Her eighth book, *The Lives of Barney Turk*, was "the story of a white youth who grew to manhood on a Florida truck farm, sought adventure in Central America, and ended up in Hollywood. The three short stories were about a Florida religious colony, a turpentine worker

at a political meeting, and a mythological hunt for the reasons
Swiss cheese has holes."[40] Her next novel, *The Golden Bench of
God*, also rejected by Scribner's, was about Madame C. J.
Walker and the hairdressing business.

III *Politics*

With her political writings, on the other hand, Zora was faring
well. In April 1950 her "What White Publishers Won't Print"
appeared in *Negro Digest,* and in November 1950, after she had
joined the conservative George Smathers group in the Smathers
versus Claude Pepper primary, another article, "I Saw Negro
Votes Peddled," appeared in the *American Legion Magazine.*
In June 1951 a second article, "Why the Negro Won't Buy Com-
munism," appeared in the *American Legion Magazine;* on December 8, 1951, *Saturday Evening Post* published her "A Negro
Voter Sizes Up Taft." When the Supreme Court announced its
famous desegregation decision in 1954, Zora responded with a
letter to the *Orlando Sentinel* (August 22, 1955). According to
her, "the whole matter revolves around the self-respect of my
people. How much satisfaction can I get from a court order for
somebody to associate with me who does not wish me near them.
. . . It is a contradiction in terms to scream race pride and
equality while at the same time spurning Negro teachers and
self-association." Zora, as did the segregationalists who later used
her letter to advantage, neglected to mention the fact that black
schools were underfunded, their facilities and resources meager.
Zora later confided to Margrit Sabloniere, a Dutchwoman interested in translating *Dust Tracks*, that "as a Negro, you know
that I cannot be in favor of segregation, but I do deplore the
way they go about ending it."[41] One must keep in mind that
Zora's point of reference, the standard by which she measured
everything/everyone, was Eatonville, a town June Jordan described as "supportive," and "nourishing . . . without exception,
her work—as novelist, as anthropologist/diligent collector and
preservor [*sic*] of Black folktale and myth—reflects this early and
late, all-Black universe that was her actual as well as her creative
world."[42] It was important to Zora that no negative, self-pitying
images of her race be allowed afoot.

Because of her impressive work with the Smathers campaign, Zora was asked to ghostwrite Smathers's father's autobiography. Zora never finished the work, ostensibly because of personality clashes with the congressman.

IV *Slave Ships in Shoes*

In the winter of 1950–51, at the invitation of friends, Zora moved to Belle Glade, Florida. In the spring, she wrote to Jean Parker Waterbury, her literary agent, that she was penniless. She had survived by "just inching along like a stepped-on worm from day to day. Borrowing a little here and there." But now the whole deal of living was becoming embarrassing, "having to avoid folks who have made me loans so that I could eat and sleep. The humiliation is getting to be much too much for my self-respect.... To look and look at the magnificent sweep of the Everglades, birds included, and keep a smile on my face."[43] Relief came when the *Saturday Evening Post* bought the Taft Article. The $1,000 made it possible for her to return to Eau Gallie to the one-room cabin where she had written *Mules and Men*. There she lived for the next five years, tending her garden, writing stories about her dogs, Spot and Shag, becoming one with her environment, enjoying a peace she hadn't known for years, in spite of recurring illnesses resulting from a "tropical fluke" contracted from impure drinking water in Honduras, a gall bladder infection and "colon and general gut" disturbances.

She wanted to buy the cabin in which she lived but her landlord was reluctant to sell because the cabin was in a white neighborhood. It was just as well; by that time Zora had no money to buy anyway.

In 1952 she became a reporter on the Ruby McCollum Case for the *Pittsburgh Courier,* writing not only an account of the trial but a biography of Ruby as well. Ruby McCollum, a fairly well-to-do black woman, had shot and killed her lover, C. Leroy Adams, a white doctor and state senator in Suwannee County. According to William Bradford Huie, whom Zora called into the case, Adams had exploited Ruby, making her his mistress only because Ruby had money. When Ruby learned that Adams, who had fathered two of her children—one already born, the other

on the way—really scorned her, she went to his office and shot
him. Though she was at first convicted of first-degree murder, the
Florida Supreme Court overturned the decision, declared Ruby
mentally incompetent, and committed her to a state hospital.
Zora's opinion of the trial is included in Huie's book *Ruby Mc-
Collum: Woman in the Suwanee Jail.*

Zora's last major literary undertaking was the story of Herod
the Great, a story which obsessed her mind and took up most
of her time. The idea for the work had been with her for years.
While aboard the *Sun Tan* in Daytona Beach, she had written
four and one-half pages to Carl Van Vechten about the story
she was "burning to write" (September 12, 1945) about the Jews.
And on July 30, 1947, she had written to him from Honduras
that she was working on a play "using the material around the
fall of Jerusalem to Titus in 70 A.D. It is a whale of a story, and
its greatness lies in the fact that it is a universal matter. The
struggle of the handful of Jews against the mightiest army on
earth, that they might be free to live their own lives in their
own way, is the struggle of democracy all over the world and
in all ages. With what is going on now, I think that it would be
a good time for it. The Romans won in the end, because the
seed of the struggle was scattered, and came at last to conquer
Rome. The symbolic Gate of Justice moved westward across the
world."[44] Ronald Cutler, professor emeritus, University of Florida,
recalls that when he wrote to Zora for a copy of "The Gilded
Six-Bits" for an anthology he was putting together, Zora responded but paid no attention to his request, the bulk of her
letter being about her Herod the Great project and how Herod
had been misunderstood.[45] Zora approached Scribner's with the
same idea, considered taking the story to Hollywood, asked Win-
ston Churchill if he would write the introduction, and even considered asking Orson Welles to collaborate, but decided that his
ego was too big.

On June 13, 1955, she wrote to Mary Spessard that she had al-
ready spent five years on Herod, three years on research alone,
and that the manuscript was two-thirds done. She hoped that
Scribner's liked the story. On December 3, 1955, she wrote to
Margrit Sabloniere that she was working on the Herod story:
"You will wonder about my choice, but he was a great and in-

fluential character of his time, and the answer to what is going on in Europe, Asia, and America lies in that first Century B.C. Besides, he was dynamic, the handsomest man of his time, a great lover, courageous to reckless, and I do not believe that any other man in public life anywhere ever lived such a dramatic life so that the epithet was applied to him "Herod of the sun-like splendor."[46] By August 1955 the die was cast. Scribner's rejected the manuscript. In September 1958 Zora, now living in Fort Pierce, inquired if the David McKay Company would be interested in Herod; they weren't. Three months later, on January 16, 1959, she wrote to the editorial department of Harper Brothers to see if it wished to see "the book I am laboring upon at present—a life of Herod the Great."[47] They didn't. The manuscript remains unpublished, in the Hurston Collection at the University of Florida.

When in the spring of 1956 her landlord in Eau Gallie decided to sell the cabin and land Zora occupied, she was forced to leave. She found work as a librarian at Patrick Air Force Base, where she stayed for almost a year, feeling the burden of her Barnard degree, which made her too conspicuous among her less educated fellow workers. On May 10, 1957, she was fired, ostensibly for having too much education for the job.

Becoming something of a transient, Zora next moved to Merrit Island across the Indian River from Cocoa. In December she was invited to write for the *Fort Pierce Chronicle*, the local black weekly in Fort Pierce, Florida. She graciously accepted, writing articles on everything from hoodoo and black magic to a story about the Tripson Dairy Co. February 1958 found her substitute-teaching at Lincoln Park Academy, the black public school of Fort Pierce.

V *Dusk*

In spite of all that has been written and conjectured to the contrary, Zora did not go hungry during these lean years, or if she did it was only long enough to gather and cook from her bountiful garden, or if there was no garden, to borrow from friends in order to buy something to eat. By 1959 she weighed in excess of an unhealthy 200 pounds. The excess weight coupled with high

blood pressure and her other recurring maladies to bring on a
stroke in early 1959. On October 29, 1959, she was forced to
enter the Saint Lucie County Welfare Home. Suffering from
"hypertensive heart disease," on January 28, 1960, she died. Her
funeral expenses were paid by family and friends, and she was
laid to rest in an unmarked grave in Fort Pierce's segregated
cemetery, the Garden of the Heavenly Rest. She was brought
to life again about ten to fifteen years ago when people like
Alice Walker and Robert Hemenway began to discover her.

As Darwin Turner has noted, Zora Neale Hurston's life "was
not the conventional rags to riches to rags melodrama. She never
attained the financial or literary riches she deserved. She reached
her peak as a writer at a time when economic depression pre-
vented Americans from buying the number of books they might
have in a more affluent period. Moreover, she did not receive as
much literary recognition as she might if she had been born a
decade earlier or later."[48]

In spite of her bad timing, however, Zora had left her indelible
mark on the world. She had become a member of the American
Folklore Society, the American Anthropological Society, American Ethnological Society, New York Academy of Sciences, the
American Association for the Advancement of Science; and she
was also listed in the 1937 edition of *Who's Who in America.*
She had been courted by political bigwigs; published four novels,
two books of folklore, an autobiography, numerous short stories,
articles; and lived a great deal.

She was to be remembered fondly by some friends and acquaintances, and not so fondly by others. After Zora's death,
Carl Van Vechten wrote to Fannie Hurst praising her for the
personality sketch she had written of Zora for the *Yale Gazette*
and reminiscing about Zora's magnetism:

I am certainly glad that I begged you to do the piece on Zora. It is
a chef d'oeuvre, a masterpiece and while I read it, I cried. You
make all the girl's faults seem to be her virtues. As a matter of fact,
they were not faults, they were characteristics. There's quite a difference. What it comes down to is the fact that Zora was put
together entirely differently from the rest of mankind. Her reactions
were always original because they were always her own. When she
breezed into a room (she never merely entered) tossed a huge straw

hat (as big as a cart wheel) on the floor and yelled "I am the queen of the niggerati," you knew you were in the presence of an individual of the greatest magnitude. You have certainly written the greatest obit I have ever read and perhaps cheered Zora in whatever department of oblivion she has chosen to reside.[49]

Robert Hemenway, Hurston's biographer, presents her as "flamboyant yet vulnerable, self-centered yet kind, a Republican conservative and an early black nationalist."[50]

No one remembers Zora better, however, than she remembers herself. No one saw her life more closely than she saw it herself. On July 5, 1941, working on the manuscript for her autobiography, she wrote:

While I am still far below the allotted span of time, and notwithstanding, I feel that I have lived. I have had the joy and pain of strong friendships. I have served and been served. I have made enemies of which I am not ashamed. I have been faithless, and then I have been faithful and steadfast until the blood ran down into my shoes. I have loved unselfishly with all the ardor of a strong heart, and I have hated with all the power of my soul. What waits for me in the future? I do not know. I cannot even imagine, and I am glad for that. But already, I have touched the four corners of the horizon, for from hard searching it seems to me that tears and laughter, love and hate, make up the sum of life.

That was her life. A picaro, she had wandered incessantly, anchoring from time to time but always casting off for farther horizons. She had soared to the skies only to fall back to earth. The glory, however, was in the trip itself; the soaring was the thing: "If you kin see the light at daybreak, you don't keer if you die at dusk. So many people ne'er seen the light at all."

CHAPTER 3

The Early Works

ACCORDING to Robert Bone (*Down Home*, 1975), "the Afro-American short story entered an authentic local-color phase in the 1920's.... Abandoning their former hopes of cultural assimilation, black writers began to place a premium on being different . . . to celebrate those differences." Not only were "the lives of the black masses accepted as a legitimate subject for the first time," but more importantly, "their speech was perceived as a powerful expression of ethnicity" instead of "a badge of social inferiority."[1] Zora Neale Hurston was very much a part of this movement to validate and authenticate the black folk experience.

Storytelling was an integral part of life in Hurston's Eatonville. The men—women were not allowed to participate—often held "lying" sessions, "straining against each other in telling folk tales. God, Devil, Brer Rabbit, Brer Fox, Sis Cat, Brer Bear, Lion, Tiger, Buzzard, and all the wood folk walked and talked like natural men."[2] Zora imbibed this tradition, stored it in her memory banks and withdrew a bit at a time to entertain people and to start her own literary career.

Almost all of Hurston's writings reflect her immersion in black folk life which, as is apparent from *Dust Tracks on a Road* and *Mules and Men*, she both lived and studied. Her short works and most of her novels are all set in southern black communities, sometimes actually identified as Eatonville, in Florida—"the roosting place of Hurston's imagination."[3] Anticipating Ralph Ellison's prescription for folklore, they reflect specific forms of humanity "found in those communities offering drawings of the group's character. [They] preserve mainly those situations which have repeated themselves again and again in the history of any given group; [they] describe those rites, manners, customs, and

56

so forth, which insure the good life, or destroy it, and [they] describe those boundaries of feeling, thought and action which that particular group has found to be the limitation of the human condition. [They] project this wisdom in symbols which express the group's will to survive; [they] embody those values by which the group lives and dies. [And although sometimes] these drawings may be crude, they are nonetheless profound in that they represent the group's attempt to humanize the world."[4]

In December 1924 Hurston launched her literary career with the publication of her first professional work, a short story, "Drenched in Light." She was in school at Howard University at the time and had submitted the story to the Urban League's magazine, *Opportunity: A Journal of Negro Life*, when the editor, Charles S. Johnson, requested material. Johnson was searching for material that would exemplify the "New Negro" philosophy that Locke would soon espouse in *The New Negro*. "New Negro" philosophy held that Blacks were full human beings (not three-quarters, as had been commonly argued), thinking persons filled with self-respect and self-dependence in contrast to the shuffling, "Old Negro" often caricatured and stereotyped in literature. Blacks now shared a common consciousness which would give rise to the black affirmation and exuberance of the Harlem Renaissance. Zora was a natural contributor, being the product of the nurturing, self-sufficient, racially proud, all-black community of Eatonville.

Johnson liked "Drenched in Light" because in expressing "New Negro" thoughts it celebrated blackness. Johnson was so effusive in his praise of the story that Hurston submitted "Spunk" which was published in June, 1925, and which Alain Locke included in *The New Negro* (1925); along with "Spunk," Zora sent a play, *Color Struck*, which was later reworked and published in Wallace Thurman's *Fire!!* By this time, Zora herself was in New York, having arrived the first week of January 1925 with "1.50 in her purse, no job, no friends, but a lot of hope."[5]

The story and the play won second prizes at an award dinner sponsored by *Opportunity* and confirmed Hurston's potential as a writer. More importantly, however, they brought her to the attention of Fannie Hurst and Annie Nathan Meyer. Hurst would

later give Zora employment, and Meyer would later give her a
scholarship to Barnard College. In January of the next year,
Opportunity republished Hurston's "John Redding Goes to Sea,"
which had first appeared in *Stylus*, the campus literary magazine
of Howard University; in August, *Opportunity* featured Zora's
"Muttsy"; "Sweat" appeared in *Fire!!* in November of the same
year; another play, *The First One*, appeared in Johnson's *Ebony
and Topaz* in 1927; and "The Gilded Six-Bits" appeared in *Story*
in 1933.

I   *"John Redding Goes to Sea"*

Though it did not appear for the scrutiny of the general public
until five years after it had appeared in the esoteric *Stylus*, "John
Redding Goes to Sea" was Hurston's first fictional work. A
groping melodramatic story of dreams deferred, of ambition,
determination, and expectations mocked to death by time, its
main character, John Redding, like Janie Crawford of *Their
Eyes Were Watching God*, anticipates the horizon, but unlike
her, never achieves it while alive. Whereas Janie's grandmother
limits her horizon to a speck, John Redding is limited by his
mother and his wife.

From his early childhood, John had known the pain of being
limited and hindered. One of his first experiences was with
twigs, which John called ships and placed on a stream to sail
away. More often than not, however, the ships would be swept
in among the weeds and held there, a foreshadowing of the
fate John himself would soon suffer. When he grew up and
wanted to explore the horizon, he was hindered by his mother
who believed that he should marry, settle down, and forget
about wandering. To Matty Redding, marriage was the solution
to everything. Perhaps to please his mother, John did marry,
but he soon began to "saunter out to the gate to gaze wistfully
down the white dusty road; or to wander again to the river as
he had done in childhood. To be sure he did not send forth
twig-ships any longer, but his thoughts would in spite of himself,
stray down river to Jacksonville, the sea, the wide world—and
poor home-tied John Redding wanted to follow them." John
quickly discovered that marriage did not make happiness; it

could not pacify that urge to wander, that quest for experience; sometimes it only brought pain and chains.

As John explained to his wife, marriage was a mistake because he could not "stifle that longing for the open road, rolling seas, for peoples and countries I have never seen." Because neither his wife nor his mother understood or encouraged him, he was a stifled free spirit, trapped in the cage of an unhappy marriage. He begged his mother to "let me learn to strive and think—in short, be a man." Ironically, though appropriately, Redding is killed in a storm and his body floats out to sea where he is free to search, explore, and realize his dreams. John Redding is a dreamer in a world which does not treat dreamers kindly. In his weakness he allows himself to be manuevered by his mother and his wife. By the time he has gathered enough fortitude to assert himself, it is too late.

"John Redding Goes to Sea," like the stories that follow it, treats many subjects that Hurston later embodies in her works. Like Isis of "Drenched in Light," Janie of *Their Eyes Were Watching God*, and Hurston as she presents herself in *Dust Tracks*, John Redding has a vivid imagination and always pictures himself on the open road. Sometimes he was "a prince, riding away in a gorgeous carriage, . . . a knight bestride a fiery charger, . . . a steamboat captain piloting his craft down the St. John River. . . . He always ended by riding away to the horizon." Like most of Hurston's male characters, John aspires to be a man, to improve himself, to be somebody. As with all dreamers, however, there are obstacles to be overcome. John only overcomes his by paying the ultimate price—his life. Sometimes, however, suggests Hurston in *Their Eyes Were Watching God*, that is the way it must be: "Ships at a distance have every man's wish on board. For some they come in with the tide. For others they sail forever on the horizon, never out of sight, never landing until the Watcher turns his eyes away in resignation, his dreams mocked to death by Time. That is the life of men."

II *"Drenched in Light"*

"Drenched in Light," Hurston's first contribution to the black literary and cultural awakening called the Harlem Renaissance,

is "a portrait of the artist as a young girl."[6] The subject is Isis
Watts, a free-spirited eleven-year-old black girl, filled with
imagination, energy, love, and vitality. Secure in self, Isis bustles
with pride, talent, and self-confidence as she searches for self-
actualization. Unfortunately, she is stifled and limited by the
restrictions imposed by her provincial grandmother.

The story is set in Florida, and focuses upon a day in the life
of Isis. From sunup to sundown, the impish Isis romps with the
dogs, turns somersaults, dances, perches upon the gatepost in
front of her home, races up and down the road to Orlando
"hailing gleefully all travelers," begging rides in cars and winning
her way into the hearts of "everybody in the country." Typically,
she gets into all kinds of mischief, even attempting at one point
to shave her grandmother's beard ("No ladies don't weah no
whiskers if they kin help it. But Gran'ma gittin' ole an' she doan
know how to shave like me.") while the old lady sleeps. When
the outside world fails to amuse, Isis turns inward to her vivid
imagination for entertainment. She wears "trailing robes, golden
slippers with blue bottons," rides "white horses with flaring pink
nostrils to the horizon," pictures herself "gazing over the edge
of the world into the abyss." She is busy making the most out
of life, much to the chagrin of her grandmother.

The only conflict in the story is caused by Grandma Potts, an
old, traditional parent who sanctions corporal punishment for
anything which goes against her seasoned principles. She thus
metes out punishment for such crimes as sitting with the knees
separated ("settin' brazen" she called it), whistling, playing with
boys, or crossing legs. Obviously there is no peace for Isis when
Grandma is around.

Grandma Potts seems to be the natural product of the slavery
tradition. When Helen, for instance, a white stranger who has
been captivated by a gypsy dance Isis performed at a local bar-
beque, her grandma's new red tablecloth draped about her
shoulder as a Spanish shawl, requests that Isis be allowed to
accompany her to her hotel to dance for her, grandma, bowing
and dissembling, happily turns her granddaughter over to the
woman. Because the grandmother does not really know Helen,
the reader at first assumes that she allows Isis to accompany her
only because the woman is white, a member of that ruling class

whom grandma has grown accustomed to obliging without question. When we are told that the grandmother is secretly bursting with pride, however, we begin to suspect that she understands and appreciates Isis's worth and only keeps up a stern front to keep the girl in line, to perhaps break her spirit (as Zora's father tried to do hers) so that she will not fall victim to a world which had little tolerance for spirited blacks. On the other hand, perhaps the grandmother was pleased because the "missus" was pleased. Isis, though ignorant of even the name of her patron, only knows that someone finally appreciates her talents, and she is happy to be rescued from a grandmother who stifles her.

Helen is sincere in her feelings for Isis; she longs for Isis's vitality. Since life has gone out of her own existence, she is determined—like the whites who hungrily flocked to Harlem during the 1920s to be liberated by the "exotic primitive"—to snatch excitement from other sources. She determines to absorb Isis's light, to live delightfully, vicariously, through Isis. When one of her male companions sarcastically suggests that Isis has adopted her as a surrogate mother, Helen is quick to reply: "Oh, I hope so, Harry . . . I want a little of her sunshine to soak into my soul. I need it."

The story is partly autobiographical and anticipates what is to come in the later works. Potts was Hurston's mother's maiden name; Isis's village seems to be Hurston's own Eatonville, and some of the events of the story are also found in autobiographical pieces written by Hurston. In a May 1928 article in the *World Tomorrow*, "How It Feels to Be Colored Me," for instance, Hurston says that as a child "my favorite place was atop the gate-post. Proscenium box for a born first-nighter. Not only did I enjoy the show, but I didn't mind the actors knowing that I liked it. . . . I'd wave at them and when they returned my salute, I would say something like this: 'Howdy-do-well-I-thank-you-where-you-goin'?'" Sometimes she would "go a piece of the way" with them. White travelers liked to hear her "speak pieces" and sing and dance and would pay her for doing those things, unaware that "I wanted to do them so much that I needed bribing to stop."[7] And she wrote in her autobiography (1942) that, as a child, "I used to take a seat on the top of the gate-post and watch the world go by. . . . Often the white travelers would hail me, but more often I hailed them, and asked, 'Don't you want me to go a piece of the way with you?' "[8] It never occurred to either Hurston or her fictional counterpart, Isis, that they were doing anything out of the ordinary. Proud and content in their blackness each wanted to improve others by bestowing themselves and their talents upon them. Robert Hemenway calls the story Hurston's "Manifesto of selfhood, an affirmation of her origins."[9] Indeed it is that, and more. By cherishing and immortalizing her memories in fiction, Hurston was seeing to it that an important part of black tradition—the folkways of her people—was not lost. The Potts family again appears in *Jonah's Gourd Vine* (1934), and *Dust Tracks on a Road* (1942); Isis, as a character, appears in *Jonah's Gourd Vine*, another autobiographical piece, as the daughter of Lucy Ann Potts and John Pearson; Isis's yearning for a vital life at eleven anticipates Janie's yearning at sixteen in *Their Eyes Were Watching God*. Like Isis, Janie is a sensitive, poetic soul in a basically unfeeling prosaic world. The dialect, infused with striking metaphors and sayings, is used to advantage in all of Hurston's novels, and the white person as deliverer or benefactor appears in *Dust Tracks* (where Hurston herself often benefits from the largesse of whites), *Jonah*, and *Their Eyes Were Watching God*.

"Drenched in Light" is undeniably Isis Potts's story. She is the heroine and subject of most of the action. Though children appear in other Hurston works, this is the only work in which a child figures significantly in the plot. The work is filled with a child's laughter, imagination, and energy. It possesses a child's charm, though it discusses more adult themes—the lasting effects of slavery and the boredom and emptiness of white adult life—in passing.

III *"Spunk"*

"Spunk," Hurston's next work, takes its title from its protagonist, Spunk Banks. The title, however, does double duty, for it not only refers to the name of the story's main character but also to his audacious attributes. The plot is a classic one of *hubris* punished, for it develops the story of a man who uses his spunk to intimidate and manipulate others, only to eventually lose his nerve and his life.

Set in a village which, though unnamed, is apparently Eaton-ville, the story is told by a narrator and by the townfolks who function as catalyst and chorus, precipitating the serious action of the story, filling in details of what happens off stage, and judging the main characters. When the story opens, Spunk has already established a reputation in the village as a hero. He is a man to be feared, "a giant of a brown skinned man," a man who "ain't skeered of nothin' on God's green footstool—nothin'!" More importantly, like the white massa, he intimidates and takes what he wants—"He rides that log down at the saw-mill jus' like he struts 'round wid another man's wife—jus' don't give a kitty." In this case, Spunk wants Lena Kanty, the wife of the town's coward, Joe Kanty. The story is based upon Spunk's desire for Lena, his realization of that desire, and the fatal consequences that arise therefrom.

When the story begins, Spunk and Lena have been together long enough for the townspeople to know of the relationship, and for Joe Kanty, the cuckolded, nervous, and cowardly hus-band, to nerve himself (i.e., gather spunk) and demand the return of his wife. Spurred and shamed by town gossip, Kanty is prompted to try a sneak attack; he confronts Banks's Army 45 with a pocket razor and dies. It is a clear case of self-defense, and no man dares dispute it. After a brief trial, Spunk is free and ready to marry Lena. Before he can do so, however, he is bothered by a big, *black* bob-cat that he cannot shoot (he believes the cat is Joe's ghost "done sneaked back from Hell!") and he claims that the saw at the mill (which he used to ride just for fun) is loose and that someone is pushing him into its blade. None of these things is happening, of course; and yet, in Poe-like fashion, they are all happening. Either Spunk's conscience and imagination are successfully working against his sanity, or a supernatural force is intervening to right the wrongs of the world. The next evening Spunk is mysteriously caught in the saw—pushed by Joe, he swears—and killed. The man of whom every-one else was afraid has brought about his own death (a natural explanation) or Joe's spirit has caused Spunk's death (a super-natural explanation). The reader must decide which. The towns-people clearly do not question the validity of the supernatural explanation. To do so is to question a very real part of the rituals upon which their society is built. In Eatonville and in many other black communities, superstitions, the supernatural, and voodoo were as common as cape jasmine bushes and sweet potatoes. At any rate, Joe seems more powerful, more *present* after his death. Perhaps, as one of the townsmen believes, Joe has been the braver man after all.

By Hurston standards, however, Kanty is not a MAN; he's one of those puny characters who are more of a nuisance than anything else. Although Banks is a MAN, on the other hand, he is a wrongheaded one, the tragic hero with too much pride who, by imposing his will upon others without proper regard for their feelings, brings about his own downfall. Too, after Spunk kills Kanty, he loses his spunk and thus becomes as cowardly and despicable as Kanty.

Ironically, Spunk Banks, who had been such a powerful man while he lived, is quickly forgotten once he is gone. Three sixteen-inch boards on saw-horses served as his "cooling board" while a dingy sheet served as his shroud. Instead of mourning his death, the townswomen "ate heartily. . . . and wondered who would be Lena's next," while the townsmen "whispered coarse conjectures between guzzles of whiskey." Life continues to flow.

Hurston explores variations of the theme of *hubris* punished in her first two novels, *Jonah's Gourd Vine* and *Their Eyes Were Watching God*. The supernatural appears in "John Redding Goes to Sea," *Jonah's Gourd Vine*, *Their Eyes Were Watching God*, and *Moses, Man of the Mountain*.

IV   Color Struck

Hurston submitted her first play, *Color Struck*, to the 1925 *Opportunity* contest along with "Spunk." Both won prizes, *Color Struck* winning second prize in the drama division. The play, though not particularly impressive as drama, is valuable for the insight it offers into intraracial color prejudice. Though the work concerns itself primarily with Florida, it chronicles the effect of a more universal phenomenon—how one's dissatisfaction with one's color can lead to inferiority complexes which undermine one's entire life. Emmaline, the play's main character, is very dark-skinned and thinks that no man can love her because her skin is so dark. When Turner, a light-skinned man, does genuinely love her, she is incapable of accepting and enjoying his love because she feels that she does not deserve it. Emmaline believes that "them half whites, they gets everything, they gets everything everybody else wants! The men, the jobs—everything! The whole world is got a sign on it. Wanted: Light Colored. Us blacks was made for cobble stones."[10]

The first three of the play's four scenes are set in "A Southern City" twenty years before the play's present action. Several blacks journey to St. Augustine, Florida, to participate in, and hopefully win, a cakewalking contest. Emmaline ruins her chances of participating in the contest when, pleading with John Turner to not enter the dance hall "cause all them girls is going to be pulling and hauling on you," she causes a rift in their relationship. John "walks" with another and Emmaline is shattered.

The fourth scene shifts to the present, twenty years later, to a one-room shack in an alley where Emmaline sits rocking, listening for sounds from her ill daughter. Turner, whom she hasn't seen for twenty years, knocks on the door, declares his love, and proposes marriage. The possibility of reunion is ruined, however, when Emmaline, afraid to leave John alone with her mulatto daughter while she goes for the doctor, waits too long and the child dies as Emmaline accuses John of lusting after the half-white body. The play is a tragedy in that because of flaws in her character, Emmaline brings about her own misery and downfall. Not only does she lose John but her daughter as well. The play is clearly a condemnation of self-deprecatory, self-defeating attitudes. It implies, in an era when "white was right," that there was nothing wrong with being black. Hurston shows here, as does Alice Walker in *The Third Life of Grange Copeland*, that often one is one's own worst enemy and that black oppression—in this case, oppression of self—can be just as stifling, just as dehumanizing, as white oppression.

V "*Muttsy*"

Written in 1925 and published in 1926, "Muttsy" was awarded one-half of second prize in the short-story section of the *Opportunity* contest. It documents the experiences of an innocent little

Red Riding Hood, Pinkie Jones, as she enters the bewildering forest of Harlem. When the story opens, Pinkie, who has journeyed North in search of refuge, has already fallen prey to the wolfish atmosphere of "Ma Turner's back parlor," a "house" run by Forty-dollars-Kate. There Pinkie feels "shut in, imprisoned, walled in with women who talked of nothing but men and the numbers and drink and men who talked of nothing but the numbers and drink and women." A gambler named Muttsy is immediately taken with Pinkie and wants to marry her. In order to win her, he gives up a lucrative gambling career for a job on the docks because Pinkie likes a man "that works for a living." A month after the marriage, however, Muttsy is on his knees with a friend shooting a perfect seven. After he has won the friend's money, he tells him to "send de others roun' heah one by one. What man can't keep one li'l wife an' two li'l bones? Hurry em up, Blue!" Pinkie has obviously, and credibly, been unable to change her husband's ways. That Muttsy has returned to his gambling does not particularly bode ill. Pinkie will probably have to modify her "likes," but a happy marriage between Muttsy and Pinkie still seems possible.

VI   "Sweat"

"Sweat" is a story of marriage gone sour, of hard work and sweat, of adultery, hatred, and death. Set in Florida (most of the action of the piece takes place on the outskirts of the town rather than in it), the story explores the relationship between a married couple, Delia and Sykes Jones, and the hatred that emanates from their marriage after love has disappeared.

Although the couple appear to be in love when they marry, Sykes soon tires of his wife—"Two months after the wedding, he had given her the first brutal beating"—and seeks companionship with various women of the town, finally settling with Bertha, a big, fat woman described by one of the townsmen as a "greasy Mogul . . . who couldn't kiss a sardine can Ah done thowed out de back do' 'way las' yeah." Delia stays home and does the laundry of white folks to earn a living for herself since her husband spends his money elsewhere. She is really the head of the household and has worked for fifteen years to pay for the house Sykes wants to give to Bertha.

When he has become so enamored of Bertha that he wishes to marry her, Sykes begins to prey upon his wife's obsessive fear of snakes. Not only does he throw his snakelike bull whip into the room to scare her, but he also pens a rattlesnake near the back door. When that is not enough to run Delia away, he moves the snake to her clothes hamper knowing that, it being Sunday, Delia will soon begin to sort the clothes for the weekly Monday washing. He hopes that the snake will kill her, thereby removing her from his sight forever. Delia escapes, however; Sykes himself is bitten—"hoist with his own petards," as it were—and dies. Delia could have warned him, saved him, but she understandably does not. She has been hardened by his constant abuse and has built up a "spiritual earthworks" against him. Poetic justice has been rendered. He had made Delia's life miserable; he had beaten her, cheated on her, and refused to provide for her. He had taken advantage of her by taking things for which she had worked and paid to Bertha's and by flaunting Bertha daringly around the community and around Delia. He had even paid Bertha's rent at Della Lewis's—"the only house in town that would have taken her in"—and promised her his wife's house. Sykes had done everything, in short, which would turn Delia, observers in the community, and the reader against him.

The story itself, however, is not as simple as the plot summary suggests. One of the reasons that Sykes cannot bear the sight of his wife, for instance, is because her work makes him feel like less than a man. He resents her working for the white folks, washing their dirty laundry, but he does not resent it enough to remove the need for her to do so. Or perhaps his wife's work has removed the need for him to be a man. Clearly Delia is an independent woman, by necessity, it seems, having worked for fifteen years to support herself and her husband, and having even paid for the house they live in. Whether she needs Sykes at all is questionable, and perhaps he senses this and looks elsewhere for someone who does need him.

Though Sykes's vulnerability and uncertainty about his own masculinity are understandable, he is still contemptible. He has not loved, trusted, understood, and appreciated Delia—a man must do these things if he is to survive in the Hurston fictional world—but has instead hated, tricked, and beaten her. As one of the townsmen noted, Sykes had "beat huh 'nough tuh kill three

women let 'lone change they looks." He is one of those men
"dat takes a wif lak dey do a joint uh sugar-cane. It's round,
juicy an' sweet when dey gits it. But dey squeeze an' grind,
squeeze an' grind an' wring tell dey wring every drop uh pleasure dat's in 'em out. When dey's satisfied dat dey is wrung dry,
dey treats 'em jes lak dey do a cane-chew. Dey throws 'em
away. Dey knows whut dey is doin' while dey is at it, an' hates
theirselves fuh it but they keeps on hangin' after huh tell she's
empty. Den dey hates huh fuh bein' a cane-chew an' in de way."
Like Spunk Banks, Sykes obviously deserves and brings about
his fate.

VII   The First One

Huston's second play, *The First One*, was submitted to the
1926 *Opportunity* contest and later printed in Charles S. Johnson's *Ebony and Topaz* (1927). The work, which "illustrates the
folkloric process by which Judeo-Christian tradition was Afro-
Americanized, the manner by which gods were made human,"[11]
is a Hurstonized account of the biblical Ham legend. Ham is
presented as a hedonist in the tradition of Tea Cake of *Their
Eyes Were Watching God* in contrast to his materialistic, prosaic
brothers, who are in the tradition of Logan Killicks and Jody
Starks, also of *Their Eyes Were Watching God*. In this, her first
attempt to dramatize biblical stories, Hurston, like the black
preacher, shows how Old Testament sagas can be Afro-Ameri-
canized and applied to everyday life. The play points out how
ridiculous it is to take seriously the biblical prescription for
racial separation and suggests that because Ham's family will
now be deprived of his company, they are the ones who have
been shortchanged. As Zora said in her *World Tomorrow* article,
"How can anyone deny themselves the pleasure of my company."[12] Though Hurston's accomplishments in this play were
slight, they were enough to suggest to her the possibilities of
fictionalizing biblical sagas, possibilities she later realized in
Moses, Man of the Mountain (1939), and which she later explored in some unpublished stories, "The Seventh Veil," and
"The Woman in Gaul."

VIII   *"The Gilded Six-Bits"*

"The Gilded Six-Bits" was Hurston's last published short story before she tried her skills with the novel. It foreshadows much of what was to come in her later works and presents the self "reconciled to its provincial origins."[13] It has more depth than the other stories, its characters are more developed, and its dialect has much of the texture we are to see in her novels. "The Gilded Six-Bits" is the most often anthologized of Hurston's works.

Set in Eatonville, "The Gilded Six-Bits" is the story of a beautiful marriage beset by difficulties, of trials and successes, of appearances and reality. Having as its theme the old adage that all that glitters is not gold, the story centers around the married life of two people, Missie May and Joe Banks, the force which tests and threatens their relationship, and their subsequent attempts to allay this force. The narrative falls logically into three parts, each of which centers around the welfare of the marriage. We see the marriage in a state of health, and in a state of ill health followed by a long, but successful, convalescence.

At first the marriage between Missie and Joe is a happy one. They show their love in small but significantly generous ways. Missie keeps a spotless home for Joe and cooks his favorite food while Joe buys her little tokens to show his love. They are so happy that there is even "something happy about the place" where they live. Their life together seems perfect, the Garden of Eden. When the serpent arrives in the form of Otis D. Slemmons, however, the Banks begin their fall.

Otis D. Slemmons is a city slicker–womanizer who sports gold teeth, a five-dollar gold piece for a stick pin and a ten-dollar gold piece for a watch charm. He and his gold impress Missie so much that she wants some of the same for her husband and takes Slemmons into her bed as a means of getting it. Although her intentions are naively good—Joe has admired Slemmons and expressed his desire to be like him—they precipitate the deterioration of the marriage.

When Joe returns home earlier than usual from work one night and catches Slemmons awkwardly trying to get into his pants,

he attacks him, accidentally grabbing the gold watch charm as
Slemmons makes a timely escape. In spite of his discovery, however, Joe remains with Missie. She becomes hopeful when Joe
makes love to her after three months of abstinence, but when
she finds Slemmon's piece of money under her pillow the next
morning, she is confused. A close examination reveals that the
money isn't gold at all, but is a gilded half-dollar. What disturbs
Missie most, however, is that Joe has left the money under her
pillow as though he were paying for her services—"fifty cents for
her love." Misery.

When Missie becomes pregnant and bears a fine boy who
resembles Joe, shadows lift and happiness once again seems
possible. Determined to let bygones be gone, Joe goes shopping
for the first time since the Slemmons incident and buys fifty cents
worth of candy kisses with the gilded money. The marriage has
come full circle, but it will never be the same. The carefree
innocence which characterized the early marriage has been replaced by painfully gained maturity and knowledge. The lesson
has been costly but because the foundation upon which the
marriage was built has been strong, the marriage has survived.
Missie and Joe genuinely love each other and both have enough
courage, determination, and trust in each other to weather the
storm. Thanks to their joint efforts, their marriage is well on its
way to recovery.

"The Gilded Six-Bits" clearly shows that the promises of the
city—to which blacks were flocking by the thousands during the
Great Migration of the early part of the century, and indeed
throughout the Harlem Renaissance—were often gilded. The
city, be it New York, Pittsburgh, Chicago (from which Slemmons
hailed), etc., promised hope and opportunity. Promises were
deferred, however; the land of opportunity became a vicious
jungle, and blacks were thrown back upon themselves. They
were able to compare the pastoral, the rural, natural folk experience with the urban experience, and they found the urban
experience lacking. Wiser and stronger, they thus became content
with their quaint folkways, found value and truth and strength
in themselves.

Significantly, four of the five stories Hurston published between
1924 and 1933 deal with marriage and marital problems, a major

theme in Hurston's works. Instead of portraying marriage romantically, however, Hurston presents it frankly, replete with infidelity, jealousy, violence, and hatred. There were certain characteristics she considered essential to a successful marriage —courage, honesty, love, trust, respect, understanding, and a willingness to negotiate differences, to prop each other up on every side. As her stories and some of her novels show, those who did not subscribe wholeheartedly to her successful marriage formula could suffer disasters.

Curiously, in the unsuccessful marriages, the male is always eliminated, i.e., killed—an unusual and hard fate—and the woman is left intact, available, as it were, for another, hopefully happier marriage. A flawed man is obviously less forgiveable in the Hurston world than a flawed woman. When the woman is at fault, however, as in "Spunk," "The Gilded Six-Bits," and *Seraph on the Suwanee*, she is made to suffer, though her punishment is mild when compared to that of the men. Lena Kanty loses both of the men in her life within a few days; Missie is taunted and tortured by her conscience and her husband for almost a year; and Arvay Henson of *Seraph on the Suwanee* torments herself throughout most of the novel, most of her life.

Though Hurston herself did not find marriage palatable—she married twice, divorced twice, after spending only a few months, maybe less, with each husband—she did advocate it highly for her characters. She recognized that for some, finding a suitable mate who will love, cherish, respect, trust, understand, and encourage is the "be-all" of life, just as she realized that for others, like herself and John Redding, marriage wasn't meant to be. In her works, she presents marriage as varied and realistically beset by hardships. To her, it was an important institution capable of various possibilities which she explores sometimes beautifully, sometimes unmercifully, but always realistically.[14]

As Bone has noted,[15] Hurston's story plots often pit the weak against the strong—John Redding against his mother, Isis Potts against her grandmother, Joe Kanty against Spunk Banks, Delia Jones against her husband Sykes, Missie and Joe against Slemmons. Though the strong may often win, however, their victory is shortlived: John's mother loses him entirely; Banks and Sykes Jones eliminate themselves; Missie and Joe's marriage weathers the storm. Hurston, as creator, will, more often than not, remove the source of the oppression and free the stifled or threatened spirit. Even "John Redding Goes to Sea" is not a sad story because John, though dead, is at last free.

Although the recognition Hurston has received has been granted almost solely on the basis of her novels and books of folklore, her short works are not to be ignored. As stories, plays, and as glosses on the novels, they mark the beginning of a career which grew to include four novels, two books of folklore, and an autobiography. More importantly, they are invaluable because they record some of the folkways of a people—"those rites, manners, customs, and so forth, which insure the good life or [as is often the case here] destroy it."[16]

CHAPTER 4

Jonah's Gourd Vine

J ONAH'S *Gourd Vine* (1934)[1] is Hurston's "story about a man."[2] The idea for the novel had come to her in 1929 while she was doing research in black folklore; between the conception of the novel and its actual publication were five trying and serious years for Hurston. She was trying to decide whether to write a book at all—"the idea of attempting a book seemed so big that I gazed at it in the quiet of the night, but hid it away from even myself in daylight"[3]—and whether, assuming she wrote, that book should be about the "Race Problem," a popular and timely subject during the 1930s:

Negroes were supposed to write about the Race Problem. I was and am thoroughly sick of the subject. My interest lies in what makes a man or a woman do such-and-so, regardless of his color. It seemed to me that the human beings I met reacted pretty much the same to the same stimuli. Different idioms, yes. Circumstances and conditions having power to influence, yes. Inherent difference, no. But I said to myself that that was not what was expected of me, so I was afraid to tell a story the way I wanted, or rather the way the story told itself to me.[4]

While Hurston was deliberating, fate was working in her favor. Bertram Lippincott, editor at Lippincott, had read Zora's "The Gilded Six-Bits" before it appeared in the August 1933 issue of *Story* and had been so impressed that he sent her a letter inquiring if she were also working on a novel. Though Zora hadn't penned a word on the book, she replied that a novel was indeed forthcoming. Using material from her own family history, she began writing *Jonah* on July 1, 1933, finished on September 6, had the manuscript typed on credit, borrowed two

73

dollars for mailing expenses from the treasurer of the local
Daughters of the Elks and sent the manuscript to Lippincott
on October 3. The book was accepted by October 16 and was
published the first week of May 1934.

The novel is about John Buddy Pearson, a likable, exasperat-
ing, bewildering character who at times resembles the Biblical
Jonah, Samson, and sometimes even Christ himself. Like Jonah,
John Buddy runs away from life, responsibility and God; like
Samson, his weakness is women and it is because of them that
he loses his strength and position of power; like Christ, he "wore
the cloak of a cloud about his shoulders. He was above the earth.
He preached and prayed," and though he sinned, "men saw his
cloak and felt it"; he draws parables, is a carpenter, and sees
himself as betrayed and wounded by his friends—one of those
that "soppeth in the dish with me"; and, though crucified, he
rises again. As a Christ figure, he is also something of a Jonah's
gourd vine who provides at least spiritual comfort to his parish-
ioners; like Christ's detractors, John's "friends" who variously
refer to him as a Jonah's gourd vine, believe that he must be
destroyed for the welfare of the community.

By endowing her protagonist with attributes of the biblical
characters, Zora lets her readers know that John Pearson, in spite
of his many shortcomings, is somebody special. In a letter to
James Weldon Johnson (April 16, 1934), she confided her intentions for the novel:

I have tried to present a Negro preacher who is neither funny nor
an imitation Puritan ram-rod in pants. Just the human being and
poet that he must be to succeed in a Negro pulpit. I do not speak of
those among us who have been tampered with and consequently
have gone Presbyterian or Episcopal. I mean the common run of
us who love magnificence, beauty, poetry and color so much that
there can never be too much of it. Who do not feel that the ridiculous
has been achieved when someone decorates a decoration. That is
my viewpoint. *I see a preacher as a man outside of his pulpit and so
far as I am concerned he should be free to follow his bent as other men*
[italics mine]. He becomes the voice of the spirit when he ascends
the rostrum.[5]

The main tension of the novel is caused by John's attempts to
live the life Hurston outlines in the letter to Johnson.

John Buddy Pearson, an illegitimate child born during slavery, lives on the wrong side of the creek with his mother and stepfather, Amy and Ned Crittendens, in Alabama after Emancipation. When he and his stepfather have irreconcilable differences, John seeks work at his mother's former home, the Pearson plantation, on the other side of the creek. While living there, he discovers his unusual susceptibility to the charms of women; knowing, however, that he actually loves only Lucy Potts, the smartest girl in his class at school, he marries her in spite of the objections of her mother who had planned for a wealthier and older son-in-law. Even Lucy, however, cannot control John's promiscuity as he ventures from one affair to another. Soon, to escape imprisonment for stealing a hog and for attacking Lucy's brother, John is forced to leave town. He wanders south to Eatonville, Florida, where his carpentry and ministry earn him a position of respect. He not only becomes mayor of the town but also moderator of the Southern Baptist Convention. Even in Eatonville, however, John cannot curb his sexual urges. When Lucy dies after a long illness, John marries Hattie Tyson, a woman of questionable morals who estranges him from his children. When John discovers that Hattie has won him via voodoo, he rebels violently, beating Hattie whenever he remembers his life with Lucy. Hattie sues for divorce, but not before winning the sympathy of the townspeople who, refusing either to hire him as a carpenter or to pay what they already owe, force John to leave Eatonville. John wanders to Plant City, where he marries a wealthy woman and slowly regains his position as a prosperous, respectable preacher. Returning to Eatonville to flaunt his possessions and strike envy in the hearts of his old enemies, he is seduced by a young prostitute; blinded by shame because of this final sin, John drives his car into the path of an oncoming train and is immediately killed.

As the plot summary shows, John Pearson is essentially a man in conflict with himself and with society. The direction of the story is determined by his insatiable desire for the flesh of women and the tension that exists between that desire and his desire for the ministry and the Word of God. The tension is essentially between the spiritual and the physical, between a man of God and the temptations of the world or the devil. On a literal level, *Jonah's Gourd Vine* concerns one man's search for spiritual equilibrium. On a broader level, however, John Pearson is a universal symbol for every man who seeks a balance between irreconcilable opposites.

John is the product of a pre-Christian society which recognizes no dichotomy between the world of spirit and the world of flesh. What Hurston gives us in *Jonah's Gourd Vine*, says Larry Neal, are "two distinctly different cultural attitudes toward the concept of spirituality. The one springs from a formerly enslaved communal society, non-Christian in background where there is really no clean-cut dichotomy between the world of spirit and the world of flesh. The other attitude is clearly more rigid, being a blend of Puritan concepts and the fire-and-brimstone imagery of the white evangelical tradition."[6] The theme of the novel— man's search for spiritual equilibrium, man's search for peace within himself—explores these attitudes and attempts to reconcile them. John Pearson's fate is so tragic, however, that the novel suggests that a successful marriage between a "formerly enslaved non-Christian communal society" which makes no clear distinction between spirit and flesh and a "fire and brimstone Puritan society of the white evangelical tradition" is impossible.

John exists in a christian society where to follow his natural bent is immoral, "an immorality arising less from personal inadequacy than from the limitations of American culture, a civilization that denies the beat of the drum, as it denies John's manhood."[7] The real tragedy of the story is that John, in spite of all of his image making and interpretations, never really discovers "the cultural dilemma that created his frustration."[8] As Nick Aaron Ford notes in *Contemporary Negro Novel* (1936), John's "rise to religious prominence and financial ease is but a millstone around his neck. He is held back by some unseen cord which seems to be tethered to his racial heritage. Life crushes him almost to death, but he comes out of the mills with no greater insight into the deep mysteries which surround him."[9]

I   *"The Jungle Track"*

As Ford has found, John's main difficulty is the invisible "cord which seems to be tethered to his racial heritage." Though like the speaker of Countee Cullen's poem "Heritage," John does not know anything about Africa, he still feels

> The unremittant beat
> Made by cruel padded feet
> Walking through my body's street,
> Up and down they go, and back.
> Treading out a jungle track.
> So I lie, who never quite
> Safely sleep from rain at night—
> I can never rest at all
> When the rain begins to fall;
> Like a soul gone mad with pain
> I must match its weird refrain,
> Ever must I twist and squirm,
> Writhing like a baited worm,
> While its primal measures drip
> Through my body, crying, "Strip!
> Doff this new exuberance
> Come and dance the Lover's Dance!"
>
>   . . .
>
> Not yet has my heart or head
> In the least way realized
> They and I are civilized.

The other blacks on the Pearson plantation are also tethered to Africa, though, unlike John, they are more successful in muffling the "padded feet/ Walking through [their] body's street." They can be African at will. At a celebration to commemorate the end of the cotton-picking season, one black declares: "Hey, you, dere, us ain't no white folks! Put down dat fiddle! Us don't want no fiddles, neither no guitars, neither no banjoes, Less clap!" (59) The narrator describes the distinctly African scene:

So they danced. They called for the instrument that they had brought to America in their skins—the drum—and they played upon it. With their hands they played upon the little dance drums of Africa. The drums of kid-skin. With their feet they stomped it, and the voice of Kata-Kumba, the great drum, lifted itself within them and they heard it. The great drum that is made by priests and sits in majesty in the juju house. The drum with the man skin that is dressed with human blood, that is beaten with a human shin-bone and speaks to gods as a man and to men as a God. Then they beat upon the drum and danced. It was said, "He will serve us better if we bring him from Africa naked and thingless." So the bukra reasoned. They tore away his clothes that Cuffy might bring nothing away, but Cuffy seized his drum and hid it in his skin under the skull bones. The shin-bones he bore openly, for he thought, "Who shall rob me of shin-bones when they see no drum?" So he laughed with cunning and said, "I, who am borne away to become an orphan, carry my parents with me. For *Rhythm* is she not my mother and Drama is her man?" So he groaned aloud in the ships and hid his drum and laughed. (59–60)

They danced to "furious music of the little drum whose body was still in Africa, but whose soul sung around a fire in Alabama. . . . Hollow-hand clapping for the bass notes. Heel and toe stomping for the little one. Ibo tune corrupted with Nango. Congo gods talking in Alabama" (60).

Though the other dancers are able to tuck Africa away until another "appropriate" time, John is not. He bases his life on the old creed; Africanisms come easily to him. When he prays in church he brings Africa to America: "He rolled his African drum up to the altar, and called his Congo Gods by Christian names. One night at the altar-call he cried out his barbaric poetry to his "wonder-workin' God so effectively that three converts came thru religion under the sound of his voice." His language is pagan poetry and he "manipulates words in order to convey to others the mystery of that unknowable force we call God."[10] As he tells Lucy, John has a knack for pagan poetry: "De words dat sets de church on fire comes tuh me jus' so. Ah reckon de Angels must tell 'em tuh me" (182). Lucy, too, loves "his primitive poetry and his magnificent pulpit gestures" (186).

The people love John as preacher because he has been untampered with by civilization and its restrictions. As Hurston says in her letter to Johnson (May 8, 1934), preachers have a "hold upon their people truthfully because they are the first artists, the ones intelligible to the masses. Like Adam Bede, a voice has told them to sing of the beginning of things."[11] This fact is brought home when John is pitted against a new preacher who

is trying to usurp John's already-crumbling throne at Zion Hope.
The Rev. Felton Cozy sits in the pulpit pompously and all during
the prayer service he takes off and puts on his "Oxford glasses."
When he gets up to preach he aims to "handle the alphabets"
and solve the race problem. His sermon is so ineffective that
he has to demand Amens and when he is finished the general
consensus is that "dat wan't no sermon. Dat wuz uh lecture"
(250). Actually Cozy is doomed before he begins because John
has preceded him with his "far-famed, 'Dry Bones' sermon, and
in the midst of it the congregation forgot all else! The church was
alive from the pulpit to the door. . . . 'Dat's uh preachin' piece uh
plunder, you hear me?' Sister Hall gloated. 'Dat other man got
tuh go some if he specks tuh top dat' " (247). Cozy doesn't "go
some," and John retains the throne, for the time being.

Even later when John preaches his last sermon for Zion Hope,
when most of his congregation is busily pushing the thorns into
his side, his poetry is so infectious that the congregation temporarily forgets its grievances and soars on the waves of his
message. This "Wounds of Jesus" sermon is so impressive that
a critic for the *New York Times* concluded that it "is too good,
too brilliantly splashed with poetic imagery to be the product
of any one Negro preacher."[12] Zora responded to the *Times* critic
in a letter to Johnson:

I suppose that you have seen the criticism of my book in the New
York Times. He means well, I guess, but I never saw such a lack of
information about us. It just seems that he is unwilling to believe
that a Negro preacher could have so much poetry in him. When you
and I (who seem to be the only ones even among Negroes who
recognize the barbaric poetry in their sermons) know that there are
hundreds of preachers who are equalling that sermon weekly. He
does not know that merely being a good man is not enough to hold
a Negro preacher in an important charge. He must be an artist. He
must be both a poet and an actor of a very high order, and then
he must have the voice and figure. He does not realize or is unwilling
to admit that the light that shone from GOD'S TROMBONES was handed
to you, as was the sermon to me in *Jonah's Gourd Vine*.[13]

When he is in the pulpit, John retains his position of awe.
To his congregation he represents far-away times, remembered

drum beats. Fittingly, at his funeral he is ushered out on the O-go-doe, the ancient African drum. "O-go-doe, O-go-doe, O-go-doe! Their hearts turned to fire and their shin-bones leaped unknowingly to the drum. Not Kata-Kumba, the drum of triumph, that speaks of great ancestors and glorious wars. Not the little drum of kid-skin, for that is to dance with joy and to call to mind birth and creation, but O-go-doe, the voice of Death—that promises nothing, that speaks with tears only, and of the past. . . . With the drumming of the feet, and the mournful dance of the heads, in rhythm, it was ended" (312).

That was the pre-Christian side of John. Most of the novel, however, is about John's attempt to cross over to the other side —to the Puritan, Christian, "civilized" side.

II   *Crossing Over*

By crossing the creek in the early pages of the novel, John is literally entering a new world. His crossing is symbolic because it represents an attempt to abandon an old world and old customs in favor of the new world and its customs. Like the blacks who migrated from the numbing, stifling South to the "promising," "emancipating" North during and after World War I, John hopes for better opportunities, a better life. Like some of the war migrants, however, he finds the ways of the new world baffling, finds acculturation next to impossible and is only metamorphosed externally. Internally he still clings to the old ways; he can not forsake them, partly because he is unaware that he should, and partly because they are a part of his blood; they give life to his existence.

Leaving the old world,

John plunged on down to the Creek, singing a new song and stomping the beats. The Big Creek thundered among its rocks and whirled on down. . . . He was on the foot-log half way across the Big Creek where maybe people laughed and maybe had lots of daughters. The moon came up. . . . Night passed. No more Ned, no hurry. John almost trumpeted exultantly at the new sun. He breathed lustily. He stripped and carried his clothes across, then recrossed and plunged into the swift water and breasted strongly over. (28–29)

He enters this new world, then, naked—like a newborn babe. Like a baby, he has much to learn, particularly since he is out of his natural environment.

Some differences between John's old world and his new one are readily apparent: back over the creek, John chopped cotton while in the new place black kids go to school; he only wore shoes when absolutely necessary while here "colored folks go around with their feet cramped up like white folks; he still calls white folks "marse" while these new folks call them mister. As one little girl snorts, "Marse Alf! Don't y'all folkses over de creek know slavery time is over? 'Tain't no mo' Marse Alf, no Marse Charlie, nor Marse Tom neither. Folks whut wuz borned in slavery time go 'round callin' dese white folks Marse but we been born since freedom. We calls 'em Mister. Dey don't own nobody no mo'." When John sees a train for the first time, he "stared at the panting monster for a terrified moment, then prepared to bolt." He is often embarrassed in this new world, often feels that he has been caught "doing something nasty." His situation is epitomized in the words of one of his tormentors: "Ah think he musta come from over de Big Creek. 'Tain't nothin' lak dat on dis side" (31).

John's initiation into this world is facilitated by his natural friendliness, his eagerness to learn, and the fact that he is Amy Crittenden's son. His greatest assistance, however, comes from Lucy Ann Potts, the wise, all-seeing girl he marries. Lucy props him up on every leaning side.

Lucy is a gourd vine to John, rescuing and protecting him from the harsh realities of life. When he is arrested for beating her brother (who actually deserves the beating and more) and for stealing a neighbor's pig in order to feed his family, he has to be rescued by Lucy who, though she has given birth only three days before, walks to the courthouse to plead for her husband. Because of her pleas, John is released in the custody of his employer who slips him $50 and recommends that he flee. John's only response to the trouble he has caused is "If Ah had uh knowed 'twuz gointer raise all dis rukus."

In Eatonville, after John has become a preacher whose extramarital affairs are the talk of his congregation, Lucy tells him how to dispel the discontent: "John now don't you go 'round dat

church mealy-moufin 'round dem deacons and nobody else.
Don't you break uh breath on the subjeck. Face 'em out, and if
dey wants tuh handle yuh in conference, go dere totin' uh high
head and Ah'll be right dere 'long side of yuh" (193). When the
rumbles are successfully squelched in conference, John naively
thinks all is well and prepares to preach "de Passover Supper in
de upper room" for the following Sunday. Lucy, however,
recommends that he replace the traditional communion sermon
with one on himself:

You preach uh sermon on yo'self, and you call tuh they remembrance
some uh de good things you done, so they kin put it long side de
other and when you lookin' at two things at de same time neither
one of 'em don't look so big, but don't tell uh lie, John. If youse
guilty you don't need tuh git up dere and put yo' own name on de
sign post uh scorn, but don't say you didn't do it neither. Whut you
say, let it be de truth. Dat what comes from de heart will sho reach
de heart agin. (196)

John does not recognize Lucy's importance in his survival
until after she is dead. When she is dying he tells her, "Ah don't
need you no mo' nor nothin you got tuh say, Ahm uh man grown.
Don't need no guardzeen atall" (204). Though he is old in years,
however, John is still a child, not fully knowledgeable in the
ways of the world. Lucy knows this, that "ignorance is de hawse
dat wisdom rides" and she warns John that "youse born but you
ain't dead. 'Tain't nobody so slick but whut they kin stand uh
'nother greasin'. . . . Don't git miss-put on yo' road. God don't
eat okra" (204). Years later, when it is much too late, John
learns the wisdom of Lucy's words. After his divorce from
Hattie Tyson, his second wife, a voodoo practitioner whom he
doesn't even remember marrying, he "was going about learning
old truths for himself as all men must, and the knowledge he
got burnt his insides like acid. All his years as pastor at Zion
Hope he had felt borne up on a silken coverlet of friendship,
but the [divorce] trial had shown him that he reclined upon a
board thinly disguised" (267). John's world "suddenly turned
cold. It was not new and shiny and full of laughter" as he had
believed when he first crossed over. No, it was "mouldy, maggoty,

full of suck-holes—one had to watch out for one's feet. Lucy
must have had good eyes. She had seen so much and told him
so much it had wearied him, but she hadn't seen all this. Maybe
she had, and spared him. She would. Always spreading carpets
for his feet and breaking off the points of thorns. But and oh,
her likes were no more on this earth! People whom he had never
injured snatched at his shoddy bits of carpet and sharpened
the thorns for his flesh" (268).

In spite of his downfall, however, John still sees himself as
innocent, his incontinence above reproach. He is still God's
chosen and anointed and sees himself as being unjustly crucified
like Christ. (His friends were sharpening the thorns for his
flesh.) On the following communion Sunday, he rejects the
traditional "Last Supper" sermon in favor of "The Wounds of
Jesus" (Zachariah 13:6), in which he likens his own wounds
to those Jesus received in the house of his friends. After his
sermon, he leaves the church without administering the communion, thereby choosing not to "soppeth in the same dish"
with those whom he feels have betrayed him. That he feels his
actions right is apparent in his explanation to his one true friend,
Hambo: "Ah don't b'lieve Ahm fitted tuh preach de gospel—
unless de world is wrong. Yuh see dey's ready fuh uh preacher
tuh be uh man uhmongst men, but dey ain't ready yet fuh 'im
tuh be uh man uhmongst women. Reckon Ah better stay out de
pulpit and carpenter fuh mah livin'. Reckon Ah kin do dat
'thout uh whole heap uh rigmarole" (282). In his first sermon in
self-defense, John had explained to his congregation that

y'all been looking at me fuh eight years now, but look lak some uh
y'all been lookin' on me wid unseein' eye. When Ah speak tuh yuh
from dis pulpit, dat ain't me talkin', dat's de voice uh God speakin'
thru me. When de voice is thew, Ah jus' uhnother one uh God's
crumblin' clods. Dere's seben younguns at mah house and Ah could
line 'em all up in de courthouse and swear tuh eve'yone of 'em,
Ahm uh natchel man but look lak some uh y'all is dumb tuh de
fack. (197)

When he can not make a living carpentering—his potential
customers act "lak dey spectin' uh house Ah build tuh git tuh

fornication befo' dey could get de paint on it"—John admits that Lucy had been wiser than he: "Lucy! Lucy! Come git me. You knowed all dis—whut yuh leave me back heah tuh drink dis cup?" He sought her "thru all struggles of sleep, mewing and crying like a lost child. . . . He was really searching for a lost self and crying like the old witch with her shed skin shrunken by red pepper and salt, 'Ole skin, doncher know me?' But the skin was never to fit her again" (285). John's gourd vine was gone forever.

When he reaches Plant City, his next resting place, however, John acquires a semblance of a gourd vine in his next wife, Sally Lovelace. Through her "proppin up" and arrangements, he not only becomes pastor of Pilgrim Rest Baptist Church but by marrying Sally he becomes part owner of her thirty houses and acquires a booming carpenter business. Sally buys him a Cadillac and new clothes, and insists that he return to Sanford to show off his wealth.

To his old acquaintances, John indeed seems to have survived the crucifixion they had given him; he had risen again in their midst. John was feeling "lak Samson when his hair begin tuh grow out agin" (295). Like Samson, however, John cannot resist womanly wiles; he knows his weakness and depends upon Sally to make him strong. She is his "guardzeen" now. On their wedding night, he "was as shy as a girl," and he told Sally that he didn't want to go to Sanford without her. He needed her protection. Out from under her shadow, he falls, succumbing to the entreaties of a prostitute. He determines to return to Sally's comfort as swiftly as the new Cadillac will take him: "Soon he would be in the shelter of Sally's presence. Faith and no questions asked. He had prayed for Lucy's return and God had answered with Sally" (309). As John muses, he is struck by a train and killed. The snake had finally found its mark.

III   Snakes in the New World

Snakes and snake symbolism abound in *Jonah*. Wherever they appear, they portend danger and evil against which John must forever be on guard if he is to survive. Although the snake often appears in its own skin, it also appears as a whip, as the people who eat away, worm-fashion, at John (whom they see as a Jonah's gourd vine), and as a train which winds and twists its way through the narrative, entrancing John with its beauty, power, and talk.

The symbolism is first subtly suggested in chapter one in the raw hide whip which Ned, John's stepfather, uses to beat his wife. Ned "uncoiled the whip and standing tiptoe to give himself more force, brought the whip down across Amy's back"(22). This scene immediately calls to mind a similar scene from the short story "Sweat." In that story, Sykes Jones uses his whip to taunt his wife who he knows is terrified of snakes. Delia is sorting clothes when "something long, round, limp and black fell upon her shoulders and slithered to the floor beside her. A great terror took hold of her. It softened her knees and dried her mouth so that it was a full minute before she could cry out or move. Then she saw that it was the big bull whip her husband liked to carry when he drove. . . . She screamed at him. 'Sykes, what you throw dat whip on me like dat? You know it would skeer me—looks just like a snake, an' you knows how skeered Ah is of snakes' "(40). Without this scene from the earlier story, Ned's whip is just a whip; with the scene, the whip becomes another taunting snake.

The snake images become stronger when John prepares to cross the creek in order to enter what he considers the land of opportunity. As Amy warns, however, crossing over has its dangers: "De Songahatchee is strong water, and look out under foot so's yuh don't git snake bit"(27). When John prepares to help the young Lucy across the branch near her house, he is warned about a cotton-mouth moccasin which frequents the area. John determines to kill the snake: "Suddenly, he snatched the foot log from its place and, leaning far back to give it purchase, he rammed it home upon the big snake and held it there. The snake bit at the log again and again in its agony, but finally the biting and the thrashing ceased"(67). This scene has its correlative in the last pages of the novel when the train rams John's body and holds it until John is dead. Just as the wounded snake thrashes here, so John's foot "twitched a little." When the snake is dead, Lucy wonders, "Reckon his mate ain't gonna follow us and try tuh bite us for killin' dis one?" John

responds that "he can't foller bofe us, lessen us go de same way."
Because Lucy and John marry, however, they do go the same
way, so the snake's mate can follow both of them; when Lucy
dies, John must go it alone; the snake's job is easier. Without
Lucy to protect him, John is subject to all kinds of sneak attacks.

Years after Lucy's death, John recalls the earlier scene in a
dream:

Lucy sat beside a stream and cried because she was afraid of a
snake. He killed the snake and carried Lucy across in his arms to
where Alf Pearson stood at the cross roads and pointed down a
white shell road with his walking cane and said, "Distance is the
only cure for certain diseases," and he and Lucy went racing down
the dusty white road together. Somehow Lucy got lost from him,
but there he was on the road—happy because the dead snake was
behind him, but crying in his loneliness for Lucy. (287–88)

John should have remembered that the snake's mate and the
danger it portends still lived. He thought the danger gone when
it had only taken another form. People and trains, as "the
greatest accumulation of power he had ever seen," could be
dangerous too.

John gets his first glimpse of a train almost immediately after
he crosses the creek when he is still a youngster. As he approaches
the town of Notasulga, "suddenly he was conscious of a great
rumbling at hand and the train schickalacked up to the station
and stopped. John stared at the panting monster for a terrified
moment then prepared to bolt. But as he wheeled about he saw
everybody's eyes upon him and there was laughter on every
face. He stopped and faced about. Tried to look unconcerned,
but that great eye beneath the cloud-breathing smoke-stack
glared and threatened. The engine's very sides seemed to
expand and contract like a fiery-lunged monster" (34–35). Right
away, John believes that the train is talking to him. He tells
one bystander, "It say something but Ah ain't heered it 'nough
tuh tell whut it say yit. . . . It say some words too. Ahm comin'
heah plenty mo' times and den Ah tell yuh whut it say" (36).

Later John notices a crude drawing of a railroad train on the
back of a songbook Lucy's brother has given him and decides
that he cannot go back over the creek with his mother, who has

come to fetch him: "No, he couldn't leave Notasulga where the train came puffing into the depot twice a day" (76).

When he is forced to leave Notasulga because of the theft and assault and battery charges, John gets his first train ride:

To him nothing in the world ever quite equalled that first ride on a train. The rhythmic stroke of the engine, the shiny-buttoned porter bawling out the stations, the even more begilded conductor, who looked more imposing even than Judge Pearson, and then the red plush splendor, the gaudy ceiling hung with glinting lamps, the long mournful howl of the whistle. . . . He marvelled that just anybody could come along and be allowed to get on such a glorified thing. It ought to be extra special. He got off the train at every stop so that he could stand off a piece and feast his eyes on the engine. The greatest accumulation of power that he had ever seen. (168–69)

During his final sermon, "The Wounds of Jesus," at Zion Hope John preaches of the damnation train:

I heard de whistle of de damnation train
Dat pulled out from Garden of Eden loaded wid cargo goin'
    to hell
Ran at break-neck speed all de way thru de law
All de way thru de prophetic age
All de way thru de reign of kings and judges—
Plowed her way thru de Jurdan
And on her way to Cavalry, when she blew for de switch
Jesus stood out on her track like a rough-backed mountain
And she threw her cow-catcher in His side and His blood
    ditched de train
He died for our sins.
Wounded in the house of His friends.
That's where I got off de damnation train. (280)

Since John sees himself as a Christ figure throughout most of the novel, it is fitting that he, too, should be rammed in the side by a train which proves to be his damnation.

In the final pages of the novel, John, in flight from his final sin, "drove on but half-seeing the railroad from looking inward. The engine struck the car squarely and hurled it about like a toy. John was thrown out and lay perfectly still. Only his foot twitched a little"(309).

IV   *Jonah*

At the center of the novel is the escape motif. Like the biblical Jonah, John Buddy is constantly trying to escape from that which demands more of him than he is willing to give. Escape is a key concept for John; the notion governs his life; running is in his blood. The motif is set in motion in the first chapter of the novel when, because of problems with his stepfather, John leaves home in pursuit of a life "over de creek" where he will be un-shackled, free to do as he chooses. Even before he crosses the creek his mother admonishes him with, "Dat's how come Ah worries 'bout yuh. Youse always uh runnin' and uh rippin' and clambin' trees and rocks and jumpin', flingin' rocks in creeks and sich like. John, promise me yuh goin' quit dat" (28). John promises but is soon playing "Hide the Switch" with the girls on the Pearson plantation on the other side of the creek. Because of his long legs he runs and overtakes them quickly. When it is time for bed, John is restless—"He could have romped till morning. In bed he turned and twisted" (41). The next night while playing "Hide and Seek," John admits that "Ah loves tuh outrun 'em and beat 'em tuh de base. 'Tain't many folks kin run good ez me"(47). When he learns that Lucy Potts is the fastest runner this side of the creek he challenges her to a race and wins. When his mother comes to take him back home to help with the sharecropping, he runs to town to hear the train's whistle which gives his feet "such a yearning for distance." When he and his stepfather quarrel, John concludes, "Shucks! Ahm goin' 'way from heah.' It came to John like a revelation. Distance was escape." "'Ahm goin' tuh zar, and dat's on de other side of far" (84–85). Back over the creek, he gets into a fight with a man over the man's wife, thinks about Lucy and the fact that she is still too young to marry him and decides to take to the road again. When he returns to marry Lucy, Pearson advises him to "Stop running away. Face things out" (113).

After John marries Lucy, he constantly runs to other women and then back again to Lucy. Taking the advice of Alf Pearson—

"John, distance is the only cure for certain diseases" (163)—he flees to Florida immediately after he has been bound over for trial in Alabama. In Florida he becomes a preacher, but not before trying to run from the charge. As he tells the church congregation, God "called me long uhgo, but Ah wouldn't heed tuh de voice, but brothers and sisters, God done whipped me tuh it" (180). Even when his daughter becomes deathly ill John flees: " 'Ah can't stand 'round and see mah baby girl die. Lucy! Lucy! God don't love me. Ah got tuh go 'way 'til it's all over. Ah jus' can't stay.' So John fled to Tampa away from God, and Lucy stayed by the bedside alone. He was gutted with grief, but when Hattie Tyson found out his whereabouts and joined him, he suffered it, and for some of his hours he forgot about the dying Isis, but when he returned a week later and found his daughter feebly recovering, he was glad. He brought Lucy a new dress and a pineapple" (190–91).

After his act of malice in which he slaps Lucy on her death bed, "John rushed from Lucy's bedside to the road and strode up and down in the white moonlight" (208). He dreams about Lucy and the snake and hears Alf Pearson telling him that "Distance is the only cure for certain diseases," and soon he is gone to Plant City. After his brief affair with a prostitute in the last pages of the novel,

he seized his coat and put it on as he hurried out to the car. Ora grabbed up her dress and dashed after him, but he was under the wheel before she left the room, and the motor was humming when she reached the running-board. John viciously thrust her away from the car door without uttering a word. He shoved her so hard that she stumbled into the irrigation ditch, as the car picked up speed and in a moment was a red eye in the distance.

The ground-mist lifted on a Florida sunrise as John fled homeward. The car droned, "ho-ome" and tortured the man. (308–309)

In this final flight, John is cut down. It was to be expected. God was bound to tire of all John's running. One is reminded of the folk song/spiritual: "Sinner man, where yuh gonna run to on Judgment Day?" Significantly, John is running back to Sally to hide—"Soon he would be in the *shelter* of Sally's presence"

(emphasis mine). There is no hiding place for John, however;
he has done his final crossing over.

V   *"The Man with No Steering Gear"*

Perhaps the most striking quality about *Jonah's Gourd Vine*
is the correlation between the novel and Hurston's early years as
she describes them in *Dust Tracks on a Road* (1942). The protagonist is John Pearson, a man whose life resembles that of
John Hurston, Zora's father, in several ways: both are Alabamians
who arrive from "over the creek" to court a girl named Lucy
Potts, the real name of Hurston's mother; both move to Eatonville to become carpenter and minister, marry a woman of
questionable morals after Lucy dies, lose favor in the town, and
die in an automobile accident. Zora even uses the deathbed
scene she remembered from her childhood when her dying
mother asked her to stop the neighbors from executing the
community ritual of removing her pillow at the moment of
passing. With so many autobiographical references, then, perhaps
the story of *Jonah's Gourd Vine* did not merely "tell itself" to
its author. Perhaps it was, in addition to being good material
for fiction, a real, though subconscious, therapeutic effort to rid
herself of her ambivalent feelings toward her father.

According to *Dust Tracks on a Road*, Hurston and her father
always had differences. John Hurston never understood his
daughter's defiance, imagination, and ambition. Such qualities,
he felt, were reserved for the white folks. He thus never encouraged her, but, instead, threw obstacles in her path. As
Hurston grew older, she began to notice her father's meandering
and how his little affairs affected her mother, Lucy Potts. Hurston
naturally resented her father for these acts. When her mother
died at a young age, just as Lucy does in *Jonah's Gourd Vine*, her
father married a shiftless woman who insisted that he put all
his children out of the house. John complied and, by doing so,
incurred Hurston's wrath. This wrath permeates *Dust Tracks
on a Road* in varying degrees as Hurston tries to decide whether
to feel sorry for her father or whether to hate him. Eventually
admitting that he was not to blame for his behavior, Hurston
decides that her father had been turned loose to hurt himself.

Because he was slow to anticipate or realize the consequences of his action, he could not prevent their effects. Hurston believed her father to be, like her protagonist, a victim rather than a criminal or offender. Having written *Jonah's Gourd Vine* eight years before her autobiography, and therein reconciled herself to her father, Hurston could say with conviction, in *Dust Tracks on a Road*, that

with my mother gone and nobody to guide him, life had not hurt him, but it had turned him loose to hurt himself. He had been miserable over the dispersion of his children when he came to realize that it was so. We were all so sorry for him, instead of feeling bitter as might have been expected. Old Maker had left out the steering gear when He gave Papa his talents. (180)

It is in *Jonah's Gourd Vine*, then, that the conflict between father and daughter is finally resolved.

It is difficult to tally all the parts of the novel—the escape motif, the snake and train symbolism, the spirit-flesh conflict, the pre-Christian–Christian/Puritan tension, the Jonah's gourd vine imagery—and come up with an acceptable, harmonious, logical sum. Both Hemenway and Darwin Turner have pointed out the shortcomings of the novel—Hurston's failure to make all parts mesh together to give some continuity to the book. Says Hemenway, "Hurston had not yet worked out a way to fictionally resolve either the bicultural tradeoffs inherent in being black in American or the relationship between the individual artist and the community that artist serves. Nor had she discovered a way to structure a novel around the image-making faculty, the suspended linguistic moment, and to sustain that structure through plot, character, setting—all the ingredients of successful fiction."[14] Turner objects most to the "Jonah's gourd vine" imagery: "The image of 'Jonah's gourd vine' does not seem to represent John effectively because no Jonah exists. The fact that John is created by God and is smitten by God furnishes merely a strained analogy."[15]

In spite of the defects pointed out by these critics, however, as a first novel written by a woman who had hidden the notion of writing a book away from herself, *Jonah's Gourd Vine* is to be commended. All of the reviewers liked it—though some obviously did not understand it—primarily because of the richness and vitality of the language, "its compelling beauty and deep compassion." Although it was not her best work, it was good enough to suggest that a classic of black literature might soon be in the making. The publication of *Their Eyes Were Watching God* one year later fulfilled all expectations. *Jonah's Gourd Vine* captures the culture of black men and women as they love and hate, dream and die in a culture-denying society. The novel is so universal, however, that its story could be anyone's, regardless of his color. The ebb and flow of life presented in the novel belongs to every person who will not or cannot reconcile himself to life. As Hemenway says, "Although the sum [of the novel] may be less than the parts, the parts are remarkable indeed."[16]

CHAPTER 5

Their Eyes Were Watching God

H URSTON'S second and best novel is *Their Eyes Were Watching God*.[1] Robert Bone called it "a classic of Black literature, one of the best novels of the period."[2] And indeed it is, bearing comparison with another literary classic—Henry James's *Portrait of a Lady*. In both novels, the protagonist is a woman who must make a major decision about the course of her life. Isabel Archer, much to the chagrin of her readers, dutifully returns to her despicable husband, Osmond, determined to lie in the cold and uncomfortable bed she has made for herself. She feels it a shirking of duty to do otherwise. Janie Crawford, on the other hand, after dutifully marrying the man her grandmother has chosen for her—an old farmer who owns sixty acres and a house— and finding no real satisfaction there, strikes out, like Huck Finn, for the territory in search of her dreams and the possibility of a better life beyond the horizon.

Her second husband is little better than her first, but Janie endures, hiding her dreams away until she is free to search again. She begins her search when she is sixteen years old. By the time she finds what she wants, she is forty. The important thing is that she never gives up the search; she simply bides her time until things get better.

Published on September 18, 1937, *Their Eyes Were Watching God* has universal implications for women in that it protests against the restrictions and limitations imposed upon women by a masculine society. Hemenway asserts that, in this novel, "Zora Neale Hurston discovered one of the flaws in her early memories of the village [Eatonville]: there had usually been only men telling lies on the front porch of Joe Clarke's store."[3] It was a society which believed that someone had to think for "women and chillun and chickens and cows" and where "men

93

saw one thing and understood ten, while women saw ten things and understood none" (110–11). Like the women of most societies, the females in Janie's town were expected and encouraged to marry for security and economic advancement.

The story is rather awkwardly told by both the heroine, Janie Crawford, and an omniscient narrator, and is revealed, for the most part, in a flashback to Janie's best friend, Pheoby Watson. The narrative is awkward in some places because much of what Janie tells Pheoby, Pheoby must already know, partly because she is Janie's best friend, and partly because Pheoby was a part of Eatonville just as Janie was. Both must have had many common experiences which there would be no need to repeat in the narrative. In order for the novel to succeed then, one must take Coleridge's advice and willingly suspend one's disbelief. Once that is accomplished, the novel succeeds handsomely.

As Hurston reveals in her autobiography, *Dust Tracks on a Road*, much of this story is based on a love she herself had experienced: "The plot was far from the circumstances, but I tried to embalm all the tenderness of my passion for him in 'Their Eyes Were Watching God.'"[4] Hemenway has discovered that the "him" was a man of West Indian parentage whom Zora first met in New York in 1931, then found again when she was in graduate school; he was a college student of twenty-three who had been a member of the cast for *The Great Day*, and was studying to be a minister. The affair was doomed from the start, partly because he could not abide her career, partly because Zora could not abide to give up her work and seemed to have a particular aversion to marriage. The only part of *Their Eyes Were Watching God* that is autobiographical, then, is the "tenderness of my passion," the "emotional essence of a love affair between an older woman and a younger man."[5] Hurston claimed that the story had been dammed up inside her, and she had released it, in seven weeks, in Haiti. What she wrote was the story of a woman in search of self and genuine happiness, of people rather than things, the story of a young, black woman with her eyes on the horizon. Although Janie Crawford's search is the main thrust of the novel, other themes—freedom from materialism, intraracial prejudice, and sex stereotyping—also demand our attention.

I   *"Marriage Lak When You Sit under a Pear Tree and Think"*

The key to the novel is Janie's idea of marriage, which is pitted against other, less romantic, ideas of marriage in the book. Janie gets her definition of marriage from nature. When she is sixteen, her sexuality awakens as she watches "the mystery" of a blossoming pear tree in her back yard: "From barren brown stems to glistening leaf-buds; from the leaf-buds to *snowy virginity of bloom*. It stirred her tremendously. How? Why? It was like a flute song forgotten in another existence and remembered again. What? How? Why?" (23). The answers to her questions come when she sees "a dust-bearing bee *sink* into the sanctum of a bloom; the thousand sister-calyxes *arch to meet the love embrace* and the *ecstatic shiver* of the tree from root to tiniest branch *creaming in every blossom* and *frothing with delight*. So this was a marriage! She had been summoned to behold a revelation. Then Janie felt a *pain remorseless sweet* that left her *limp and languid*" (24; italics mine). The sexual imagery in these passages is blatant. The scene is orgasmic and impresses Janie so strongly that she experiences "a pain remorseless sweet" after which she is "limp and languid." This is the idea of marriage that she carries with her and for which she searches for nearly thirty years. It is a romantic notion, certainly, but one certainly worth harboring.

After she witnesses the "marriage" between the pear tree and the bee, Janie looks for similar marriages elsewhere. She finds what she seeks inside the kitchen of the house where she lives with her grandmother: "In the air of the room were flies tumbling and singing, marrying and giving in marriage" (24). This, too, is nature at work. Janie identifies with the pear tree; all she needs is the right dust-bearing bee to pollinate her buds. Then she will be happy: "Oh to be a pear tree—any tree in bloom! With kissing bees singing of the beginning of the world! She was sixteen. She had glossy leaves and bursting buds and she wanted to struggle with life but it seemed to elude her. Where were the singing bees for her?" (25). That the intensity of her desire would blind her to reality is made ironically and immediately apparent in the very next paragraph where Janie, looking "through pollinated air saw a glorious being coming up the road. In her former blindness she had known him as shiftless Johnny Taylor, tall and lean. That was before the golden dust of pollen had beglamored his rags and her eyes" (25).

As a blossoming pear tree, Janie remains "petal open" for love. Before she is properly pollinated, however, she is desecrated many times.

II Desecrators of the Pear Tree

The desecrators come in the form of the people whose notions of marriage differ drastically from Janie's but not from each other's. Janie's grandmother and Janie's first and second husbands all see marriage as a materialistic security venture. They limit Janie and spit on her pear tree image.

Nanny Crawford, Janie's grandmother, sees marriage as a "way out" for Janie, as escape from poverty and abuse, a chance to sit on "a high place." Nanny's greatest wish is that Janie find a respectable husband with property so that she can avoid the traditional fate of black women—"De nigger woman is de mule uh de world so fur as Ah can see. Ah been prayin' fuh it tuh be different wid you. Lawd, Lawd, Lawd!" (29). "Ah can't die easy," she tells Janie, "thinkin' maybe de menfolks white or black is makin' a spit cup outa you" (37). A product of slavery, Nanny understandably wants something different and better for her granddaughter than the servile role women were forced to play, and the illegitimate half-white children they were often forced to bear. To Nanny, being married is being like white folks: "You got yo' lawful husband same as Mis' Washburn or anybody else!" (40). So, in an attempt to make her granddaughter "like white folks," Nanny chooses Logan Killicks as her granddaughter's husband. It does not matter to Nanny that Killicks is middle-aged, dirty, unloving, and looks "like a skull-head in the graveyard"; all that matters is that he has sixty acres, "de onliest organ in town, amongst colored folks," a house bought and paid for, and he offers protection:

'Tain't Logan Killicks Ah wants you to have, baby, it's protection. Ah ain't gittin' ole, honey. Ah'm *done* ole. One mornin' soon, now, de angel wid de sword is gointuh stop by here. De day and de hour

is hid from me, but it won't be long. . . . Mah daily prayer now is
tuh let dese golden moments rolls on a few days longer till Ah see
you safe in life.(30)

By choosing Killicks as a husband for her granddaughter,
Nanny makes two errors. Darwin Turner describes the first:
"Feeling that life cheated her by enslaving her, Nanny vows that
her granddaughter will enjoy the happiness she herself has never
known. But seeking to realize herself through her granddaughter,
she fails to allow for Janie's personality and aspirations."[6] As
Nanny tells Janie: "Ah wanted to preach a great sermon about
colored women sittin' on high, but they wasn't no pulpit for
me. . . . Ah been waiting a long time, Janie, but nothin' Ah been
through ain't too much if you just take a stance on high ground
lak Ah dreamed." When Janie complains that she does not love
Killicks and can see no way to love him, she discovers what
Nannie means by "a stance on high ground": "You come heah
wid yo' mouf full uh foolishness on uh busy day. Heah you got
uh prop tuh lean on all yo' bawn days, and big protection, and
everybody got tuh tip dey hat tuh you and call you Mis' Killicks,
and you come worryin' me 'bout love" (41). Janie asserts herself and her wishes when she replies: "Ah ain't takin' dat ole
land tuh heart neither. Ah could throw ten acres of it over de
fence every day and never look back to see where it fell. Ah feel
de same way 'bout Mr. Killicks too. Some folks never was meant
to be loved and he's one of 'em" (42). To ease her grandmother's
mind, Janie does return to Killicks; she is, however, only marking
time.

Nannie's first error naturally leads to her second. Because
she wants to live through Janie, to obtain through her the things,
the protection and security she herself never had, she is blinded
to Killicks's shortcomings. Actually Killicks is too set in his ways
and obsessed with his property to treat Janie like a real woman;
instead, he treats her like the livestock on his farm; he soon
measures her value, then, in terms of how much work she can
do and how much time she spends doing it. Ironically, Janie
has become something of a "spit cup" after all; her role is
hardly more than servile. Fearing that Janie is more of a liability
than an asset, Killicks tells her: "If Ah kin haul de wood heah

and chop it fuh yuh, look lak you oughta be able tuh tote it inside. Mah fust wife never bothered me 'bout choppin' no wood nohow. She'd grab dat ax and sling chips lak uh man. You done been spoilt rotten" (45). To insure that he gets returns on his investments in Janie, Killicks purchases a second mule that is "all gentled up so even uh woman kin handle 'im." Though Janie might have progressed from being the "mule of the world," she cannot escape the mule altogether, it seems. Flight seems to be her best option, and since her grandmother has died a few months before, Janie needn't worry about "letting her down easy."

Killicks, like Nanny, is obsessed with materialism, with things rather than with people. Robert Bone describes Janie's life with Logan Killicks, her first husband, and Jody Starks, her second husband, as an unnatural commitment to "prose" (materialism) and her life with Tea Cake, her third husband, as one of loving devotion to "poetry" (the "folk culture" and sensual "intensity").[7] The "prose," however, as James R. Giles points out, "is closer to a puritan sense of duty which is unnatural to Janie and her world because it more correctly belongs to white people, and the "poetry" is actually a primitive form of hedonism which Miss Hurston is associating with Blacks."[8] Hemenway elaborates: "People erred because they wanted to be *above* others, an impulse which eventually led to denying the humanity of those below. Whites had institutionalized such thinking, and black people were vulnerable to the philosophy because being on high like white folks seemed to represent security and power. Janie's grandmother [and Jody Starks] thinks that freedom is symbolized by achieving the position on high."[9]

III   *"Something to Drape Her Dreams Over"*

Janie finds another bad catch in her next husband, Jody Starks, an ambitious young man on his way to make his fortune in the small, all-black community of Eatonville, Florida. To the romantic Janie, he is a knight in shining armor for he not only rescues her from her miserable marriage with Logan, but he also offers to fulfill her dreams if she will run away and marry him. Janie is reluctant to accept Jody's offer because he "did not represent sunup and pollen and blooming trees" (50). Because he "spoke for far horizon" (50), however, she capitulates.

When Starks comes to fetch her in his hired rig, Janie unties the apron, a symbol of her servile life with Killicks, from around her waist, and takes a seat beside Starks: "With him on it, it sat like some high, ruling chair. From now on until death she was going to have flower dust and springtime sprinkled over everything. A bee for her bloom. Her old thoughts were going to come in handy now, but new words would have to be made and said to fit them" (54–55). Unfortunately, Janie does not have the presence of mind that she needs to read Starks correctly. That Starks, who reminds Janie of Mr. Washburn, transforms the rig into "some high, ruling chair" and has already told her that "A pretty doll-baby lak you is made to sit on de front porch and rock and fan yo'self" (49) should have given Janie pause. She, after all, does not wish to sit on high and be ruled. Starks does represent far horizon, however, so Janie becomes Mrs. Jody Starks, later Mrs. Mayor Starks. Naive and trusting, she is petal open for him.

Some critics, who are perhaps too steeped in cold reality, have pointed out that Hurston has her heroine acquire a second husband here without benefit of a divorce from her first. According to Janie, however—and by extension, according to Hurston— her marriage with Killicks was never consummated: she was petal open but he was no pollen-bearing bee; the only dust he brought was field dirt and most of that was on his feet. Janie had complained to Nanny that "His belly is too big too, now, and his toe-nails look lak mule foots. And 'tain't nothin' in de way of him washin' his feet every evenin' before he comes tuh bed. 'Tain't nothin' tuh hinder him 'cause Ah places de water for him. Ah'd ruther be shot wid tacks than tuh turn over in de bed and stir up de air whilst he is in dere" (42). Janie did not, could not, love Killicks and thus could not "froth with delight"; no orgasm was forthcoming, so obviously no marriage had taken place—not by Janie's pear tree standards, at any rate. As Hurston says in the second paragraph of the novel, for women "the dream is the truth [the sole reality]. Then they act and do things accordingly." Figuratively, then, Janie is still in "snowy virginity of bloom." With Killicks, she "waited a bloom time, and a green time and an orange time. But when the pollen again gilded the sun and sifted down on the world she began to stand around the gate and expect things. . . . Her breath was gusty and short. . . . The familiar people and things had failed her so she hung over the gate and looked up the road towards way off. She knew now that marriage did not make love. Janie's first dream was dead, so she became a woman" (43–44).

Janie's new husband becomes mayor of Eatonville and, as proprietor of the general store, its wealthiest citizen. Jody Starks, consumed by ambition and a desire for property and possessions, soon begins to treat Janie like a showpiece: "Jody told her to dress up and stand in the store all that evening. Everybody was coming sort of fixed up, and he didn't mean for nobody else's wife to rank with her. She must look on herself as the bell-cow, the other women were the gang" (66). And he forbids her to participate in the main entertainment of the town, the telling of "lies" around the porch of the community store: "You'se Mrs. Mayor Starks, Janie. I god, Ah can't see what uh woman uh yo' 'sability would want tuh be treasurin' all dat gum-grease from folks dat don't even own de house dey sleep in. 'Taint no earthly use. They's jus' some puny humans playin' round de toes uh Time" (85).

Starks obviously believes that women are to be seen and not heard. When the people of the community ask for "uh few words uh encouragement from Mrs. Mayor Starks," Mayor Starks is quick to reply: ". . . Mah wife don't know nothin' 'bout no speech-makin'. Ah never married her for nothin' lak dat. She's uh woman and her place is in de home" (69). Janie, being the individual that she is, takes silent exception to her husband's attitude; it took "the bloom off of things." As far as Starks believes, Janie is incapable of such a "masculine" attribute as thought. He himself is too caught up with egotism and self-elevation to think about her except as a possession. As Ellease Southerland diagnoses, Jody's "ambition is powerful enough, but his love [is] short-sighted."[10] He is too busy building a big, white mansion—a high place which he thinks will represent security and power—which makes the rest of the town look like servants' quarters. It is no mistake that he often prefaces his remarks with "I, god." His attitude makes "a feeling of coldness and fear take hold of [Janie]. She felt far away from things and lonely" (74).

When she is twenty-four and has been married seven years to Jody, Janie closes her petals; her relationship with her husband becomes purely perfunctory: "The spirit of the marriage left the bedroom and took to living in the parlor. It was there to shake hands whenever company came to visit, but it never went back inside the bedroom again.... The bed was no longer a daisy-field for her and Joe to play in. It was a place where she went and laid down when she was sleepy and tired" (111). When Jody slaps her one day when dinner turns out badly,

Janie stood where he left her for unmeasured time and thought. She stood there until something fell off the shelf inside her. Then she went inside there to see what it was. It was her image of Jody tumbled down and shattered. But looking at it she saw that it never was the flesh and blood figure of her dreams. Just something she had grabbed up to drape her dreams over. In a way she turned her back upon the image where it lay and looked further. She had no more blossomy openings dusting pollen over her man, neither any glistening young fruit where the petals used to be. She found that she had a host of thoughts she had never expressed to him, and numerous emotions she had never let Jody know about. Things packed up and put away in parts of her heart where he could never find them. She was saving up feelings for some man she had never seen. (112)

Not only does Jody prohibit Janie from talking with "the common folks," but he demands that she wear a head rag to hide her beautiful hair when she works in the store. Parts of the real Janie, then, are all wrapped up, literally and figuratively.

Jody Starks is too much like Logan Killicks to make Janie happy. Starks, like Killicks, feels that Janie ought to be proud and grateful for what he has done for her. After all, he has lifted her out of the valley and placed her on his mountaintop:

Here he was just pouring honor all over her; building a high chair for her to sit in and overlook the world and she here pouting over it! Not that he wanted anybody else, but just too many women would be glad to be in her place. (98)

Janie, though humble, is not grateful. She doesn't want to be above anybody. She just wants to be equal.

The years took all the fight out of Janie's face. For a while she thought it was gone from her soul. No matter what Jody did, she said nothing. She had learned how to talk some and leave some. She was a rut in the road. Plenty of life beneath the surface but it was kept beaten down by the wheels. Sometimes she struck out into the future, imagining her life different from what it was. But mostly she lived between her hat and her heels, with her emotional disturbances like shade patterns in the woods—come and gone with the sun. She got nothing from Jody except what money could buy, and she was giving away what she didn't value. (118)

Janie's position, however, is only temporary until the opportunity she awaits presents itself. In the meantime, having considered flight and rejected it ("To where? To what?" [118]), she becomes a stoic: "She got so she received all things with the stolidness of the earth which soaks up urine and perfume with the same indifference" (119). Things climax about sixteen years later when Janie, who has been constantly and publicly reminded of her aging by Jody, decides to strike back. The scene is the store and the results are a short version of the dozens[11] with the fatal blow being levied by Janie: "Humph! Talkin' 'bout me lookin' old! When you pull down yo' britches, you look lak de change uh life" (123). Jody is shattered:

Janie had robbed him of his illusion of irresistible maleness that all men cherish, which was terrible. The thing that Saul's daughter had done to David. But Janie had done worse, she had cast down his empty armor before men and they had laughed, would keep on laughing. When he paraded his possessions hereafter, they would not consider the two together. They'd look with envy at the things and pity the man that owned them. When he sat in judgment it would be the same. Good-for-nothings like Dave and Lum and Jim wouldn't change place with him. For what can excuse a man in the eyes of other men for lack of strength? Raggedy-behind squirts of sixteen and seventeen would be giving him their merciless pity out of their eyes while their mouths said something humble. There was nothing to do in life anymore. Ambition was useless. (123–24)

Janie has shown Jody that the security and power of the "high place" is largely an illusion. Shortly afterwards, Jody, now broken, takes to his bed. Within a few weeks he is dead. He dies pretending to believe that he has been "fixed" by his wife. As stated in Chapter 2, to be "fixed" by someone was not an uncommon belief among blacks during the early twentieth century. Hurston had introduced voodoo and its powers in "Spunk," *Jonah's Gourd Vine* (1934), and *Mules and Men* (1935). The implication is that the supernatural—voodoo, in this case—exercises its powers, whenever summoned by voodoo practitioners, over natural man. Although Joe Starks does not really believe that he has been "fixed" by his wife, then, its possibility is seriously considered by the other townspeople.

Although Janie hasn't used voodoo against her husband, she is finally free. She had run off from her first husband to keep house with Jody "in uh wonderful way. But you wasn't satisfied wid me de way Ah was. Naw! Mah own mind had tuh be squeezed and crowded out tuh make room for yours in me" (133). Jody's death gives her another chance. Just as she had thrown the apron away when she left Killicks so she could now throw the head rag away which had been a symbol of her imprisonment with Jody. She could once again let down her hair and try to live. Having discovered that "she had an inside and an outside now and . . . how not to mix them," she sends her "starched and ironed face" to Joe's funeral, but she herself "went rollicking with the springtime across the world" (137). The horizon is before her once again, and this time Janie does not plan to let it out of her sight.

All of her life, Janie has been searching, but thus far she hasn't found. She is interested in people and love while all the people who have controlled her life thus far—her grandmother, Logan Killicks, and Jody Starks—have been interested in property and wealth, and the respectability each seemingly brings. They have insisted upon prose (materialism), while Janie herself prefers and seeks poetry.

Having tried her grandmother's way of life, Janie now determines to live her own. She explains to Pheoby:

[Nanny] was borned in slavery when folks, dat is black folks, didn't sit down anytime dey felt lak it. So sittin' on porches lak de white madam looked lak uh mighty fine thing tuh her. Dat's whut she wanted for me—don't keer whut it cost. Git upon uh high chair and sit dere. She didn't have time tuh think whut tuh do after you got up on de stool uh do nothin'. De object wuz tuh git dere. So Ah got up on de high stool lak she told me, but Pheoby, Ah done nearly languished tuh death up dere. Ah felt like de world wuz cryin' extry and Ah ain't read de common news yet. (172)

She hates her grandmother for limiting her to a speck when the whole horizon beckoned:

She had been getting ready for her great journey to the horizons in search of *people*; it was important to all the world that she should find them and they find her. But she had been whipped like a cur dog, and run off down a back road after *things.* . . . Here Nanny had taken the biggest thing God ever made, the horizon—for no matter how far a person can go the horizon is still way beyond you—and pinched it in to such a little bit of a thing that she could tie it about her granddaughter's neck tight enough to choke her. She hated the old woman who had twisted her so in the name of love. (138)

As for her husbands, since Janie insisted upon being petal open with them, it was essential that they be open and communicative with her. That was not the case, however, both Killicks and Jody refusing to share themselves; they did not know how. When Janie suggested to Killicks that she might run off and leave him someday, Killicks refused to reveal his real feelings: "There! Janie had put words to his held-in fears. She might run off sure enough. The thought put a terrible ache in Logan's body, but he thought it best to put on scorn. 'Ah'm gettin' sleepy, Janie. Let's don't talk no mo'. 'Tain't too many mens would trust yuh, knowin' yo' folks lak dey do' "(51). Jody, on the other hand, had insisted that Janie wear a head rag, but he "Never told Janie how jealous he was. He never told her how often he had seen the other men figuratively wallowing in it [her hair] as she went about things in the store. . . . She was there in the store for *him* to look at, not those others. But he never said things like that. It just wasn't in him (86–87). When Jody overheard Janie expressing sympathy for an abused mule which often served as the butt of many jokes, he bought the mule, turned him loose to pasture, and to become everyone's favorite. He never told Janie, however, that he had bought the mule to please her. By contrast, after Janie meets Tea Cake, he quickly tells her to "Have de nerve tuh say whut you mean" (165). While Janie had been forced to tuck herself away with her first two husbands, with Tea Cake, "her soul crawled out from its hiding place" (192).

IV "A Glance from God"

The second part of Janie's life deals with its poetry, with trying to know "the common news" so she'd be ready for the "extry" when it came. When Tea Cake (whose real name is Vergible Woods), a happy-go-lucky black man at least eighteen years younger than Janie, arrives in town, Janie's springtime begins a new growth. Tea Cake, in contrast to Janie's first two husbands, worries very little about money or material posessions; instead, he plays the banjo, hunts, plays checkers, and gives mammoth parties. Unlike Killicks who had "desecrated the pear tree" and Starks who didn't represent "sun up and pollen and blooming trees," Tea Cake could be "a bee for her bloom." He is not interested in Janie's fortune, as the townspeople believe (they, too, subscribe to the prosaic code), but finds her attractive as a person capable of infinite thought, emotion, and imagination. He accepts her for herself and as an equal. Tea Cake lives only for the moment. Giles compares him to the *paisanos* in Steinbeck's *Tortilla Flat*—the "primitives" who live only for love, fighting, and a glass of wine."[12] All this is not to suggest that Tea Cake, in his incessant pursuit of pleasure, lacks a sense of reality and responsibility. He is generally dependable and provides everything Janie wants and needs. Tea Cake makes her feel alive, vital, needed, wanted, loved, and unlimited, and she gives of herself freely. The horizon, with all its infinite possibilities, is back. Tea Cake promises happiness, and happiness it is. Janie forgets her age in her newfound youth. She is a young girl again watching the bees "marry" the flower blossoms. Her blossom is open and Tea Cake is definitely her bee. Finding the town too confining for their ever-increasing love, Janie and Tea Cake leave town, become man and wife, and set up frenetic but

blissful housekeeping. Janie dons overalls and she and Tea Cake
work side by side picking beans in the muck of the Florida
Everglades. And while Tea Cake can not offer the security or
ambition of the first husbands, he brings her the joy of simple
things in many simple ways. Their bliss lasts, with the usual
periods of fleeting distrust and jealousy, for about two years.
Then a storm hits the Everglades, and God takes his glance away.

V *"Their Eyes Were Watching God"*

During the storm, God seems to be speaking. The river dikes
are overflowing and "the lake was coming." Caught in the eye
of the storm, Janie and Tea Cake are forced to await the out-
come. They wait on God to make His move. When destruction
seems imminent, Janie and Tea Cake strike out for higher ground.
They make it, but not before Tea Cake, in an effort to save Janie,
is bitten by a mad dog. Not knowing that the dog has rabies,
however, Tea Cake does not see a doctor but instead, after the
storm has abated, returns to the Everglades. He gradually becomes more and more irrational, keeping a loaded pistol under
his pillow and periodically pulling it out to aim at Janie. When
he can not swallow water, he suspects that Janie is responsible
and believes that she is trying to kill him so that she can marry
Mrs. Turner's brother. When he actually fires at Janie, she returns
the shot, killing Tea Cake as his teeth close in the flesh of her
arm. As "a glance from God," Tea Cake has been temporary:
"The Lord giveth, and the Lord taketh away."

That he should die here, in precisely this way, seems melodramatic, unlikely, and unprepared for. There is no artistic justi-
fication for the use of rabies and its particular symptoms as the
cause of death. Rather, they seem a convenient, though uncon-
vincing, tool to eliminate Tea Cake and to bring us back to the
reality of Janie Woods and her story. For some unexplained
reason, Janie must return alone to Eatonville. Tea Cake has
given her happiness, but, like all happiness, it has been transitory,
and it has been costly. Having accomplished his purpose—to
make the realization of Janie's dreams possible—his physical
presence seems no longer required. His death is unreasonable,
but, as a key passage of the novel emphasizes,

all gods dispense suffering without reason. Otherwise they would
not be worshipped. Through indiscriminate suffering men know fear,
and fear is the most divine emotion. It is the stones for altars and
the beginning of wisdom. Half gods are worshipped in wine and
flowers. Real gods require blood. (215–16)

As a matter of course, a trial is held to determine Janie's innocence or guilt in the shooting of Tea Cake. Many of Tea Cake's
friends find Janie guilty in their own minds, but the all-white
court finds her innocent. She had acted in self-defense. Alone
now, exonerated, distraught, and bereaved, Janie buries Tea
Cake in grand style—she herself continues to wear her overalls—
reconciles herself to his friends, and returns to Eatonville. When
she walks back into the town she had left only two years before,
the townspeople, making "burning statements with questions,
and killing tools out of laughs," wonder about her overalls. Janie
has felt no need to discard them; unlike the apron and the head-
rag, the overalls have represented emancipation, life, poetry. It
is appropriate that they should replace the blue satin dress she
had worn when she left the town.

It was there in Eatonville that the horizon had beckoned when
Tea Cake entered her life. She has seen and thoroughly explored
that horizon. It has brought memories that she will never forget.
Tea Cake represented intensity and experience. As Janie views
their relationship, she has "been a delegate to de big 'ssociation
of life" (p. 18). Tea Cake, of course, is not dead, not really. He
could never die as long as she herself lived:

He could never be dead until she herself had finished feeling and
thinking. The kiss of his memory made pictures of love and light
against the wall. Here was peace. She pulled in her horizon like a
great fish-net. Pulled it from around the waist of the world and
draped it over her shoulder. So much of life in its meshes! She
called in her soul to come and see.(286)

Giles suggests that "Janie will now develop a new method of
coping with time—reflective hedonism. She will cultivate memories of sexuality and drama. She needs no new experience because
her cup is full."[13]

On the simplest level, Hurston's novel is about a woman who

knows the value of love and who determines, despite her many errors, to settle for nothing less. On a higher level, however, Hurston's novel has implications for anyone with a dream who perseveres in spite of overwhelming obstacles until that dream is realized. It is about the universal quest for the fulfillment of body and soul, for it makes clear that material possessions and security are not really the stuff out of which good marriages and love are made. Born in a racial, masculine environment which expected certain stereotyped reactions from women, especially if they happened to be black, Janie becomes larger than her world, embracing the horizon as the limit, and throwing off the shackles of womanhood and society. She attempts to survive within society at first, as her two early marriages attest, but determines to please herself when tradition fails to satisfy her.

VI *Reality*

As much as Hurston probably wanted it to be, her novel, beautiful though it is, is not all about a woman's quest for, and discovery of, self and love. Though this theme does loom large in the novel, there are racial overtones which suggest the social tension of the southern scene, tension felt in a fleeting, though profound, way. There are three cases in point. The first is bedded in the past of Janie's grandmother. Nanny, like many other attractive female slaves, had to suffer the sexual whims of her white master. The natural result was an illegitimate child who strongly resembled her white father. The master's wife resented Nanny and her child and threatened to torture her to death. The guilty master, meantime, had gone to fight in the Civil War. Nanny evaded the white woman's revenge by escaping with her child and hiding in the swamps until Emancipation was proclaimed. Her experiences with the burdens of slavery colored her ideas about women and the uses men made of them. No wonder, then, that she wanted something better for Janie, some security so that Janie would not be at the whim of any man, be he white or black.

Because of the nature of her experiences with the white world, Nanny becomes the chief spokesman for prosaic materialism. After running away with her illegitimate child, she had been taken in by a kind, white lady, Mrs. Washburn. When Nanny's daughter matured, however, she was raped by her school teacher and she, too, bore an illegitimate child—Janie. Although Nanny was not responsible for her own sexual transgression—she was forced by her white master—she did feel that her daughter was responsible for hers. And she felt it poor repayment for the kindness of their white benefactress. Thus, since Nanny's entire moral code has developed in reaction to white pressure, she longs for that white moral respectability she has never had. She sees Janie as her last chance to achieve this respectability, and she uses her accordingly.

The second racial incident is manifested in the behavior of Mrs. Turner, a light-complexioned black woman with Caucasian features and a hankering for whiteness. She idolizes Caucasian traits in others and despises Negroid characteristics. She thus feels honored by Janie's acquaintance and is taken aback when she learns that Janie loves blacks:

You'se different from me. Ah can't stand black niggers. Ah don't blame de white folks from hatin' 'em 'cause Ah can't stand 'em mahself. 'Nother thing, Ah hates tuh see folks lak me and you mixed up wid 'em. Us oughta class off.... And dey makes me tired. Always laughin'! Dey laughs too much and dey laughs too loud. Always singin' ol' nigger songs! Always cuttin' de monkey for white folks. If it wuzn't for so many black folks it wouldn't be no race problem. De white folks would take us in wid dem. De black ones is holdin' us back.... Look at me! Ah ain't got no flat nose and liver lips. Ah'm uh featured woman. Ah got white folks' features in mah face. Still and all Ah got tuh be lumped in wid all de rest. It ain't fair. Even if dey don't take us in wid de whites, dey oughta make us uh class tuh ourselves. (210–11)

Viewing regression toward blackness with horror, Mrs. Turner, like the blue-veined society of Chesnutt's "The Wife of His Youth" and Wallace Thurman's *Blacker the Berry*, believes that light-skinned black people should first seek union with whites; or, if this is impossible, should establish a separate and distinct mulatto caste. She has obviously been brainwashed into thinking that white is right, and she behaves accordingly. Her thinking is akin to that of mulatto characters presented in early black novels: like them, she disregards snubs and ill treatment, grovels before whiteness, and simultaneously subjects dark folks to insult and humiliation. She wants Janie to get rid of Tea Cake and marry her brother. Janie, who has been affirming blackness, is puzzled by Mrs. Turner: "We'se uh mingled people and all of us got black kinfolks as well as yaller kinsfolks. How come you so against black?"

The third racial case occurs during the aftermaths of the Lake Okechobee hurricane when the white leaders of the community demand that all white storm victims be buried in pine boxes while black victims were simply to be heaped together and covered with quick lime. Although a kind of racial tolerance had seemed to prevail during the crisis, it was now clear that whites did not want even dead black bodies near the bodies of dead whites, even though death itself knew no discrimination. As Ellease Southerland asserts, the novel "does not ignore realities."[14]

The novel's main thrust, however, is toward life, toward affirmation rather than denial. "Janie's strength gives power to the novel so that, in spite of the hard times and the death, the novel speaks for life."[15] It speaks for the self, for equality, for the pursuit of happiness instead of possessions; it speaks for, and seems to recommend, a way of life uncluttered by tradition, stereotypes, materialism, and violence. While Richard Wright's *Native Son* (1940) was denying life and its possibilities, Hurston's novel was affirming life, suggesting that all that is beautiful and necessary can be found among the folk. Unquestionably, says June Jordan, *"Their Eyes Were Watching God* is the prototypical Black novel of affirmation; it is the most successful, convincing, and exemplary novel of Blacklove that we have. Period." But, continues Jordan,

the book gives us more: the story unrolls a fabulous, written-film of Blacklife freed from the constraints of oppression; here we may learn Black possibilities of ourselves if we could ever escape the hateful and alien context that has so deeply disturbed and mutilated our rightful efflorescence—*as people*.[16]

Even though the novel concludes, then, with Janie returning from burying her lover, the novel does not overwhelm the reader with a sense of tragedy and protest. Rather,

... a lighter mood develops, not so much from Miss Hurston's emphasis upon a philosophic acceptance of grief as from her admixtures of comedy and her tendency to report dramatic incidents rather than to involve the reader with the emotions of the characters.[17]

Janie's dream of love had been deferred for a long time, but because of her determination, patience, and persistence, her dream did not explode; rather, it blossomed into a vital reality, and therein lies the undeniable power of *Their Eyes Were Watching God*, a novel about a woman with her eyes on the horizon.

When Janie returns to Eatonville, she is an older and wiser woman. She has learned that even the best things must end, but she has enjoyed herself immensely. She has no regrets. She no longer cares about the community and its gossip: "If God don't think no mo' 'bout 'em than Ah do, they's a lost ball in de high grass" (16). She has realized her dreams and she is content to settle back and enjoy the memories. And, although she still does not esteem material possessions, she has come to realize their value. Because she still owns the house Jody Starks built in Eatonville, she has a home to return to. And because she has money in the bank, a more comfortable existence is possible. Materialism—prose—then, has its place, for after the ecstatic, creative, and poetic storm is over, a calm prevails which brings reality back into its proper perspective. Dreams, after all, are not the sole reality. That is the lesson Janie Starks must learn, and she learns it slowly but well. The opening paragraph of the novel explains the problem with dreams:

Ships at a distance have every man's wish on board. For some they come in with the tide. For others they sail forever on the horizon, never out of sight, never landing, until the Watcher turns his eyes away in resignation, his dreams mocked to death by Time. That is the life of a man. . . . For women, the dream is the sole reality. . . . (9)

By the end of the novel, however, even Janie's dream has been "mocked to death by Time." And, like all dreamers, she can only watch in resignation with an overwhelming sense of her own helplessness. She must accept another reality. Janie still has no regrets. Though the price has been high, she has lived the better life:

We been tuhgether round two years. If you kin see de light at daybreak, you don't keer if you die at dusk. It's so many people never
seen de light at all. Ah wuz fumblin' round and God opened de
door. (236)

"Dusk" inevitably must come, but enough "light" (sexuality,
dramatic existence), explains Giles, lessens its power. It was all
right for Tea Cake to die young, then, for, although sensual
pleasure and a dramatic existence are no ultimate defense against
death, they at least mitigate death's victory.[18] Tea Cake and
Janie have lived a full life. Neither has any regrets. Janie has
stored up enough experiences to withstand the loss.

CHAPTER 6

Moses, Man of the Mountain

ALTHOUGH Hurston fails to mention *Moses, Man of the Mountain*[1] in her autobiography, she did write it somewhere between 1937, when *Their Eyes Were Watching God* was published, and November 1939, when *Moses, Man of the Mountain* was published. The seed for the story had been planted in one of her short stories, "Fire and Cloud" (*Challenge*, September 1934), which describes a dead Moses sitting upon his own grave on Mount Nebo explaining to a lizard how, amidst strife and tribulations, he delivered the Hebrews from bondage. *Moses, Man of the Mountain* is perhaps the most intriguing and ambitious of the Hurston works for it combines fiction, folklore, religion, and comedy in a daringly provocative, unusual manner. Such a mixture would inevitably cause problems and often Hurston is hard put to reconcile all these elements to produce a perfect blend. Darwin Turner calls the novel Hurston's "most accomplished achievement in fiction," adding that "if she had written nothing else, Miss Hurston would deserve recognition for this book."[2] Turner is right in saying that Hurston deserves recognition for this book, but is effusive in calling it her "most accomplished achievement in fiction," a compliment reserved for *Their Eyes Were Watching God*. Turner seems to later realize his mistake when, in terms that seem to contradict his earlier praise, he says: "The chief art of the book is abundant comedy. . . . But a good joke, at best is merely a joke. Miss Hurston's joke entertains readers but does not comment significantly on life or people."[3] Turner is not totally accurate here, either, for *Moses, Man of the Mountain*, though comic in places, is much more than a good joke and does comment seriously and significantly upon both life and people. The only critics who

113

seem to have recognized the real merit of the novel are Blyden Jackson, Ann Rayson, and Robert Hemenway.

Jackson praises the novel for its objectivity and universality:

In such art as this an artist pilots himself through the right purgatory. He loses the dross of a personal self. The steps Miss Hurston takes are all objectifications of a point of view under the proper auspices. She herself, in becoming the exponent of her Negro folk, ceases to be Zora Neale Hurston. Her Negro folk, in becoming the transparent other selves for Biblical personalities, rise above the level of their own subjectivity even while they sacrifice not one whit of their local charm. And her novel in dissolving itself with a main stream of Western tradition, gives pleasing evidence that a transcript of Negro life need not be parochial, but may anchor securely its substratum in the universal mind.[4]

Rayson, on the other hand, calls *Moses, Man of the Mountain* unique because it does two things. First, it "continues the character development of the Southern black preacher-womanizer with a gift for oratory and charm. Secondly, [it] reintroduces the theme of petty men versus real men," and is thus "a natural outgrowth of *Jonah's Gourd Vine*."[5] Although Rayson acknowledges the humor in the book, she accounts for it by saying: "The characters only appear ridiculous because of the historical solemnity associated with them in most other depictions."[6] The humor is purposeful, of course, and though the novel does veer between parody and serious fiction, "Hurston's introduction indicates that she is attempting a realistic portrayal of the Moses story of pagan and Christian traditions."[7]

Robert Hemenway, Hurston's biographer, offers praise and censure. At one point he lauds *Moses, Man of the Mountain* as one of Hurston's "two masterpieces of the late thirties,"[8] explaining that "Hurston acts as a tradition-bearer for an Afro-American worldview, simulating the process of creation that had led to the spirituals, reaffirming the act of imagination that could make Moses African rather than Hebrew, a conjure man instead of a mere conduit for divine power. She identifies with the creativity that could make slaves a chosen people in the midst of a culture structured to deny them a sense of special status."[9] At another point, however, Hemenway calls the novel "a noble failure" because "its author could not maintain the fusion of black creative style, biblical tone, ethnic humor and legendary reference that periodically appears."[10] As a result, the reader is hard put to decide what his proper response to the novel and its characters should be. The humor often seems ill placed and clashes with rather than relieves the solemnity of the occasion. "Nevertheless," concludes Hemenway, "the book fascinates, making *Moses, Man of the Mountain* one of the more interesting minor works in American literary history."[11]

The story itself, as its title implies, is Hurston's version of the Moses legend, retold with a few significant departures from the biblical original. Missing is the long, interpolated portion between the middle of Exodus and the last of Deuteronomy in which an anonymous character speaks at length about the laws, restitution, ritual, and Hebrew genealogy. Everything else is essentially intact: the Hebrews are in captivity; Pharaoh refuses to let them go; Moses is reluctant to become involved, but does so at the command of God and the incessant urging of Jethro, his mentor and father-in-law; under the pressures of plagues, Pharaoh agrees to let the slaves go, but reneges each time the pressure is removed; Moses eventually leads the Hebrews to the Promised Land, stopping enroute at Mount Sinai to receive the Ten Commandments from God; the Hebrews tarry in the wilderness to ready themselves for Canaan; and so on. What Hurston has done with this legend, however, makes the novel interesting and unique. Almost irreverently, she has infused the old story with new life, giving the Hebrew slaves an authenticity they lack in the solemn biblical story. Her role as narrator here is much like that of the Afro-American preacher who interprets "the beginning of things" to the multitudes. In *Moses, Man of the Mountain* Hurston renders into language the reader can understand the story of Moses and the Israelites. Her updated modern version gives the biblical story a compelling immediacy.

What Hurston has done is to make the Hebrew slaves American Negroes before the Civil War. This technique, of course, is an established tradition in oratory, sermons, and literature: Dunbar's "Ante-bellum Sermon," Baldwin's *Go Tell It on the Mountain*, W. E. Turpin's *O Canaan!* (where Chicago equals the promised land), Wright's "Fire and Cloud," Roark Bradford's

Ole Man Adam and His Chillun, Marc Connelly's *Green Pastures*,[12] and any other literature in which American slaves are likened to the children of Israel, the South becomes Egypt, and/or the First Migration is likened to Exodus.

To achieve the kind of distance she needed to comment objectively upon the question of slavery, Hurston transplanted American blacks to, and acclimatized them within, an Old Testament milieu. Instead of the solemnity characteristic of the biblical Hebrews, "a beastial [sic] sensuality and intelligence, coupled with the shrewdness of the market place, surrounds Hurston's characters."[13] We become suspiciously aware of this when we see the Hebrew workmen in Egypt working for the "bossman," and when we hear Jochebed—the mother who tries to protect her male baby by placing him in a basket on the Nile—speaking to the river: "Nile, youse such a great big river and he is such a little bitty thing, show him some mercy please" (39). In the wilderness, the people of Israel, grown tired of manna, long for the diets they enjoyed back in Egypt: ". . . the nice fresh fish . . . nice sweet-tasting little pan-fish . . . [of which] a person could get all they could eat for five cents—and the nice fresh cucumbers, and the watermelons, and the leeks and the onions . . . [the] garlic for seasoning" (308)—diets, in short, which were often attributed to black folk.

Not only do the language and diets give the novel a distinctive Negro folk flavor, but the housing situation in Goshen also strongly resembles the big house-shanty habitats characteristic of plantation days. Pharaoh, of course, lives in his palace (the equivalent of the huge white mansions of the agrarian South), while the Hebrews live in hovels which strongly resemble the cabins from plantations of the antebellum South.

Interestingly, God as a character does not figure largely in this reproduction of the biblical saga. Whereas He is overwhelmingly present, handing down laws and directions, in the Bible, He seldom appears in Hurston's domestic version. He appears to Moses as the burning bush on Mount Horeb and to the Hebrews as the pillar of fire which goes before them wherever they go. He talks with Moses on Mount Sinai and dictates the Ten Commandments to him. Moses, however, is the center of attraction in the book. While God is God of the Mountain, Moses

is the Man of the Mountain and, it seems, a much more interesting character. To the Israelites, Moses is their God. It is
almost as if Hurston does not want to press the issue of whether
there is a God or not. He seems to be in her novel mostly because
He is in the Bible, her source book for the novel. In her autobiography, she tried to decide about God. She was only able
to conclude, however, that,

having looked at the subject from many sides, studied beliefs by
word of mouth and then as they fit into great rigid forms, I find I
know a great deal about form, but little or nothing about the mysteries
I sought as a child. As the ancient tentmaker said, I have come out
of the same door wherein I went.

But certain things have seemed to me to be true as I heard the
tongues of those who had speech, and listened at the lips of books.
It seems to me to be true that heavens are placed in the sky because
it is the unreachable. The unreachable and therefore the unknowable
always seems divine—hence, religion. People need religion because
the great masses fear life and its consequences. Its responsibilities
weigh heavy. Feeling a weakness in the face of great forces, men
seek an alliance with omnipotence to bolster up their feeling of
weakness, *even though the omnipotence they rely upon is a creature
of their own minds.* It gives them a feeling of security. . . .[14]

These are strange statements, of course, coming from the
daughter of a Baptist minister. They are not so strange, however, coming from a believer in, and practitioner of, voodoo.
Actually, Hurston seemed to believe in Hoodoo, the religion of
Moses, and the Baptist evangelism of her father's preaching.
As Evelyn Helmick comments, "Her soul was large enough to
embrace them all."[15]

Hurston's God, then, leaves most of his work to Moses. And,
strangely enough, Moses seems to have acquired most of his
supernatural skills not from God but from other, more worldly,
sources. He has the rod that turns into a serpent and a blooming
walking stick, and he has that powerful right hand. The rod
is clearly a gift from God, but that right hand—well, that is
another story. When he leads the chosen, Moses does so "amidst
reservations, clouds of self-doubt, naivete, and the brash heroism
of a confidence man."[16] He tells Pharaoh for instance "I'd let them

children of Israel go if I were you, but don't let *me* over-per-
suade you." When Aaron tells him that he thinks Pharaoh is
ready to do his bidding, Moses responds: "I hope not. I want to
show that man a thing or two!" After he had led the Hebrews
to the Red Sea only to be swiftly pursued by Pharaoh and his
army, Moses "laughed to himself as he thought, Pharaoh thinks
he's pursuing me, but it's the other way around. I been on his
trail for thirty years, and now I got the old coon at last. . . . Let
me fuddle him all up for a night and then I will raise my hand.
First and last, I'm showing him my ugly laugh" (234).

I *Moses*

Not only does Hurston delve into Moses's childhood—an omission in the biblical version—but she also demystifies him and
presents him as the most powerful god in the black folk culture,
indeed "the finest hoodoo man in the world." To the traditional
Christian concept of Moses—"Moses was an old man with a
beard. He was the great law-giver. He had some trouble with
Pharaoh about some plagues and led the children of Israel out
of Egypt and on to the Promised Land" (7)—Hurston adds:

Asia and all the Near East are sown with legends of this character.
. . . Then Africa has her mouth on Moses. All across the continent
there are the legends of the greatness of Moses, but not because
of his beard nor because he brought the laws down from Sinai. No,
he is revered because he had the power to go up the mountain and
to bring them down. Many men could climb mountains. Anyone
could bring down laws that had been handed to them. But who can
talk with God face to face? Who has the power to command God
to go to a peak of a mountain and there demand of Him laws with
which to govern a nation? What other man has ever seen with his
eyes even the back part of God's glory? Who else has ever commanded the wind and the hail? The light and darkness? That calls
for power, and that is what Africa sees in Moses to worship. For he
is worshipped as a god. . . .
So all across Africa, America, the West Indies, there are tales of
the powers of Moses and great worship of him and his powers.
But it does not flow from the Ten Commandments. It is his rod of
power, the terror he showed before all Israel and to Pharaoh, and
THAT MIGHTY HAND. (7–8)

Unfortunately, Hurston never resolves the tension between the conjurer Moses and the Moses of the bible, the law-giver and emancipator. As a result, Moses seems extremely holy and mysterious at times; at other times, he seems extremely worldly, impulsive, tempestuous, a regular braggadocio, running his game on those who cross him.

Hurston discounts the biblical version of Moses's origins, presenting it as a mythical concoction of Miriam, the daughter of a Hebrew couple, Amram and Jochebed, to get herself out of a tight spot. According to Hurston legend, Miriam had actually fallen asleep while watching the basket containing her brother on the Nile, and when she awoke to find that "child and his basket were gone, that was all," she had invented the story that the princess had taken the baby to the palace to raise as her own. Despite the lack of corroborative evidence, the story had spread quickly, and become legendary. "Men claimed to have seen signs at the birth of the child and Miriam came to believe every detail of it as she added them and retold them time and time again. Others conceived and added details at their pleasure and the legends grew like grass." The Hebrews want to believe that "we is kinfolks to Pharoahs now" and that they have played a dirty trick on their oppressors, gotten the upper hand after all: "Ho, ho! Pharaoh hates Hebrews does he? He passes a law to destroy all our sons and he gets a Hebrew child for a grandson. Ain't that rich." The story functions much like the Afro-American folk tale where Blacks, unable to triumph over whites in reality, triumph over them in their minds and in their literature: "The crowd talked far into the night of the Hebrew victory over Pharaoh and went home. They did not question too closely for proof. They wanted to believe and they did. It kept them from feeling utterly vanquished by Pharaoh. They had something to cherish and chew on, if they could say they had a Hebrew in the Palace" (50–51). That the princess had taken the baby is unlikely; she did take a casket from the Nile, which Miriam told herself contained "the things for washing the Princess" (42). When Jochebed presents herself at the palace gate to offer to nurse the child, she is informed that there is no new baby to be nursed. Later, however, Moses's radical activities lend credence to the rumor. As chief of the Army, he demands that the slaves be included in the forces of

Egypt, but is opposed, naturally, by most of the court. Moses's wife and his uncle begin to question his birth and years later even Moses himself considers the possibility of being a Hebrew. To Hurston, however, Moses was clearly an Egyptian.

It seems ironic that the great leader of Hebrews is not himself a Hebrew—the irony is compounded by the fact that the reader is never sure if Moses is white or black—and it brings the question of motive to bear on the story. Why, after all, would a member of the ruling class—a liberal, who may be unwittingly passing —wish to help the peasants, especially when he has very little if anything to gain, and everything to lose, including his life? The answer Hurston offers is that Moses is a MAN, a good man, who, unlike his peers, is not interested in money, position, and personal gain. Instead, he is interested in people, in human life, in justice, and he feels it his calling to help those less fortunate than he. Moses doesn't need to be a Hebrew to feel and to do all this. All he needs to be is a man.

Moses began preparation for his mission while he was still a child at court. Unusually wise, inquisitive, and imaginative, he studied diligently, learning from Mentu, an old stableman employed around Pharaoh's castle, all about animals and the languages they speak. From observing the palace priests, he discovered how to master people by distracting their minds "from their real troubles," and tainting them "with the fear of life." From the book of Thoth, recommended by Mentu, he learned how to enchant the heavens, earth, abyss, mountains and sea; how to understand the birds and creeping things and how to understand "the secrets of the deep." His greatest and most influential teacher is the Midianite Jethro, seemingly God's emissary, who teaches Moses how to emancipate the children of Israel.

II   *"The Big Job"*

After Moses's abilities and knowledge surpass Jethro's, Jethro informs Moses that he is ready for "That big job I been saving up to get done over forty years. . . . Those people, I mean those Hebrews, need help, Moses. And besides, we could convert 'em, maybe. That really would be something—a big crowd like that coming through religion, all at one time" (155–57). Moses, like

Jonah and like John Buddy Pearson of *Jonah's Gourd Vine*, rejects
his mission at this point, explaining that "I don't want to be the
preacher. . . . I just want to practice up on all this new stuff
I done learned" (157).

Actually, however, Moses had been unwittingly preparing for
"the big job" all along. While in Egypt, he had killed an Egyptian
foreman for beating an already bloody slave, and he had "found
a new sympathy for the oppressed of all mankind" (92). He had
suggested to Pharaoh that the Hebrews be allowed to serve in the
Egyptian army, and all the studying he had done was really a
readying of his mind to tackle the monumental task. When he
fled Egypt because he feared his crime would be revealed and
because his birthright was being seriously and maliciously ques-
tioned in the palace, "He was wishing for a country he had never
seen. He was seeing visions of a nation he had never heard of
where there would be more equality of opportunity and less difference between top and bottom." He was seeking a place, in
short, where there were no rulers and slaves, where all were free
and equal. Even though he didn't know it yet, Moses was to help
create this ideal nation. In crossing the Red Sea, thereby imposing self-exile, he had taken a giant step toward the fulfillment of
his dreams. The narrator records the significance of Moses's flight:

Moses had crossed over. He was not in Egypt. He had crossed over
and now he was not an Egyptian. He had crossed over. The short
sword at his thigh had a jewelled hilt but he had crossed over and
so it was no longer the sign of high birth and power. He had crossed
over, so he sat down on a rock near the seashore to rest himself. He
had crossed over so he was not of the house of Pharaoh. He did not
own a palace because he had crossed over. He did not have an
Ethiopian Princess for a wife. He had crossed over. He did not have
enemies to strain against his strength and power. He had crossed
over. He was subject to no law except the laws of tooth and talon.
He had crossed over. The sun who was his friend and ancestor in
Egypt was arrogant and bitter in Asia. He had crossed over. He felt
as empty as a post hole for he was none of the things he once had
been. He was a man sitting on a rock. He had crossed over. (103–104)

As Hemenway points out,

this is a passage about identity, in a book exploring group identity, and it illustrates how Zora Neale Hurston always had at creative command the black American esthetic tradition—a tradition best represented by the forms growing from folk expression. Humor here derives from the pun on *passing* (crossing over the color line) and the reversal of the normal direction for crossing (usually one passes for white). There is historical irony that Moses can cross the Red Sea not as a miracle, but as a result of a natural parting of the waters from the action of the tide. But the passage refers most profoundly to the difficult process of constructing a new identity from the ground up, with no blueprints to predict the final shape of the edifice. Moses' life will be *transformed* into something entirely new when he comes to identify with the oppressed; he truly crosses over into a new and different land, one that will subject him to the "laws of tooth and talon." His religion will change from that of the Egyptian gods of the sun to that of the Hebrew god of the mountain. It is, of course, a religious metaphor that Hurston is using, referring to the crossing over from the sinner's bench to the amen corner, from the heathen to the saved, from the state of the unregenerate to that of the elect. It also has a secular context, referring to the crossing over from slavery to freedom. Like a black minister exhorting his congregation to cross over into a *new* life *in* Christ, Hurston's prose not only uses the phrases, but also captures the repetitive pattern and rhythm of the folk sermon—leaving one to gasp for breath and interject the rhythmic *aaaah* of the black preacher after each "he crossed over."[17]

The passage also brings to mind the concern of Johnson's protagonist in the *Autobiography of an Ex-Coloured Man*, who wonders if "I have sold my birthright for a mess of pottage," and it reminds one of what blacks often found when they "crossed over" to freedom in the North—deferred dreams, stifled hopes, harsh realities—"the laws of tooth and talon," slavery conditions without benefit of the small pieces of salt pork (fat back, it was called), greens, and corn meal. Because Moses is figuratively gradually journeying from "the North" to "the South," he, of course, is electing the condition of the oppressed, including the fat back, greens, and corn meal.

His sojourn in Midian where he meets Jethro and Zipporah, who becomes his second wife, may be seen as a kind of tarrying, a readying of the body and the spirit for battle. He flees his

mission but simultaneously prepares for it. He is sidetracked by
his desire for Zipporah but once that is placed in its proper perspective, he prepares to do battle. He practices his art by causing
small, relatively harmless, plagues in Midian, and he perfects that
right hand. He comes to believe and accept what Jethro tells him:
"I know now that the God of the mountain has been waiting for
you. . . . You are a hundred times my superior. The great I AM
took the soul of the world and wrapped some flesh around it and
that made you. You are the one being waited for on this mountain. You have the eyes to see and the ears to hear. You are the
son of the mountain. The mountain has waited for the man"
(137). After Moses talks with God via the burning bush on
Mount Horeb, he tells Jethro, "I am a man that has been
called" (165).

III   *"My People, My People"*

The "abundant humor" of the novel that Darwin Turner refers
to is part and parcel of Hurston's seemingly irreverent view of
the biblical legend—the result of the juxtaposition of a historical,
solemn occurrence with a modern-day, dialect-filled insolemnity.
The attitudes of the Israelites are enough to try Job's patience.
When the Egyptian foreman whom Moses killed in the slave's
behalf, is replaced with a Hebrew, the slaves reveal the ubiquity
of intraracial strife: "I don't intend to let no Hebrew boss me
around" because "He ain't no better than I am" (94). This attitude, of course, suggests that the slaves do feel that the Egyptians are somehow better than they and are thus deserving of
their positions as rulers. Hurston had explored this self-defeating
attitude at length in *Jonah's Gourd Vine* where John Pearson,
defeated by his enemies, is told that "Our people is jus' lak uh
passle uh crabs in uh basket. De minute dey see one climbin' up
too high, de rest of 'em reach up and grab 'em and pull 'im back.
Dey ain't gonna let nobody git nowhere if dey kin he'p it" (263).
In his prestigious position as pastor and moderator, John had
blindly believed the world to be "new and shiny and full of
laughter." He had painfully discovered, however, that this was
not so: the world was "mouldy, maggoty, full of suck-holes—one
had to watch for one's feet. . . . People whom he had never injured

snatched at his shoddy bits of carpet and sharpened the thorns for his flesh" (268). From the Hebrews' ungrateful reactions, Moses quickly learns that "It costs you something to do good! The will to humble a man more powerful than themselves was stronger than the emotion of gratitude. It was stronger than the wish for the common brotherhood of man. It was the cruelty of chickens—fleeing with great clamor before superior force but merciless towards the helpless" (95). He later tells Jethro: "I'm through trying to regulate other folks' business. There ain't no future to it at all—just a whole lot of past. If you find a cow stuck in the mire, and pull her out, she'll hook you sure" (157).

The truth of these insights is brought home to Moses when, telling the people of Goshen to pack and get ready to leave Egypt, he is "hooked for sure":

"Good gracious! I was figuring on going fishing tomorrow morning. I don't want to be bothered with no packing up today. It's too much like work and I just got free this morning."

. . .

"Looks like we done swapped one bossman for another one. I don't want nobody giving me no orders no more." (224)

Each time trouble arises, the Hebrews long for slavery back in Egypt. When the Egyptians decide that they want their slaves back, for instance, and pursue Moses and his train, the cries from the crowd are numerous:

"I always told my husband not to bother with this mess. I tried to tell him we was getting along all right under the Egyptians. But he was so hard-headed he had to go and get mixed up in it. (232–233)

"Couldn't that man find graves enough in Egypt to bury us all without dragging us out here in the wilderness to die?" (233)

"I told you all a long time ago that we had enough gods in Egypt without messing with some fool religion that nobody don't know nothing about but Moses. You all just let him make a fool out of you. I always knowed it was some trick in it. That man is a pure Egyptian and Pharaoh is his brother. He just toled us off so his brother could butcher us in the wilderness. I told you all so."

"Who asked him to butt in nohow? Our business didn't concern

him, did it? It was our backs they was beating. It wasn't none of his,
we was satisfied he ought to been tickled to death. Now Pharaoh
is going to kill us all.(233–34)

Similar cries go up from the Children of Goshen every time
trouble threatens and every time a new whim arises for something different. As Joshua tells Moses, his people "was under the
impression that you had found some god who was going to save
us. They didn't know you had to join the army."

When the slaves' suspicious, ungrateful, and light attitudes
are juxtaposed with the solemnity and seriousness of Moses, the
result is twofold: first a light ironic humor prevails and second,
the realization that the slaves are clearly not ready for the Land
of Canaan is brought painfully home; the tarrying in the wilderness forty years is absolutely necessary. There must be time for
self-actualization, for throwing off the bondman's attitude and
appreciating individual worth. The Hebrews must prepare to
liberate themselves, for as Moses painfully learns, "Freedom was
something internal. . . . All you could do was to give the opportunity for freedom and the man himself must make his own
emancipation." Joshua has every reason to shake his head and
mutter, "My People! My People. . . . My people just won't do."

Although the Hebrews in general complain constantly, two
"upstarts" in particular worry Moses about making significant
changes tailored to the two of them. These two are Aaron and
Miriam, who claim to be the brother and sister of Moses. Because these two are both haughty and feel that they should be
distinguished for being "the very ones that got this thing together
and kept it together all down the line," they are brought down
by Moses. Miriam is finally so under his power that she has to
ask his permission to die and Aaron has to be stripped of his
priestly robes and killed. Moses's killing of Aaron on Mount Hor
is one of the few departures in plot from the story of Exodus.
By making such a change, Hurston seems to be saying that this
is the real story behind Aaron's death—he is killed by Moses to
keep him from disgracing himself; thus he becomes a saint. In
the Bible, Aaron dies on the mountain and is not nearly as
arrogant and deserving of punishment as he is here. Here, of
course, he seems more representative of that group which

struggles to acquire power. About himself and his strategies, Aaron says: "I got too much brains for people. You don't meet my kind every day. I let folks think they are using me for a tool when all the time I'm using them for a step-ladder" (329). When Moses reminds him of God's decree that all the old folks who came out of Egypt, with the exception of Joshua and Caleb, had to die in the wilderness, Aaron responds with:

Oh, I never took much stock in that, Moses. I'm not the people, you know. I believe I'm going to make it and when I do, I mean to be folks over there. The thought of it has kept me living or else I would have gone like Miriam. She fretted herself to death about who was going to get us there. That was foolish. I let who can get us there, then we can see about things after that. I know how to handle people. (331)

The deaths of Aaron and Miriam were extremely painful for Moses. He had wished and prayed for better, but there had been no easier way. Miriam and Aaron, like the majority of the Israelites, had hindered the movement more than they had helped it.

All the Israelites were a people who found it difficult to believe that life could be different and better for them. They were afraid of the unknown; real freedom for them seemed impossible. When left to their own devices they reverted to the old familiar ways. For instance, when Moses ascended Mount Sinai to receive the Ten Commandments from God, the erstwhile slaves returned to their old gods and built a golden calf to worship. In a ceremony reminiscent of the African celebration in *Jonah's Gourd Vine*, they oiled their bodies and danced in ecstasy:

The thing shook Israel like a wind. Suddenly the camp came alive. . . . "A real old down home Egyptian ceremony getting ready to come off with Aaron at the altar. Just like old times back home. And they tell me a breakdown and stomp is going to follow." (283)

At the end of the forty years in the wilderness, however, the Israelites were finally ready to enter the Promised Land. As Moses reasoned,

He had given Israel back the notes to songs. The words would be according to their own dreams, but they could sing. They had songs and singers.

They might not be absolutely free inside, but anyway he had taken from them the sorrow of serving without will, and had given them the strife of freedom. He had called to their memories the forgotten words of love and family. They had the blessing of being responsible for their own. (346)

The Israelites, then, in spite of, if not because of, their pettiness were to be pitied. In a number of instances they were their own "massas" in that they retained their slavery mentality even when they were no longer slaves. They felt incapable of leading themselves and even after the generations of growth before they approached Jordan, they still offered Moses a kingship:

The people had missed the whole point of his forty-odd years of work. He loved freedom and justice with a fierce love and he wanted Israel to be free and just. All that he had done to them and for them was intended to bring them to his viewpoint. And here they were wanting to be like other halted people that they touched along the way. They despised their high destiny. They misunderstood him so far that they even offered him a crown! (327)

On the other hand, in spite of their bickering, the Israelites had rallied to their cause. They had fought and conquered when it had been necessary, and they had produced Joshua, who "had all those big virtues that command respect, and all those commonplace vices that make men understood. Men congregated about him. They respected his virtues and admired his vices. So he became the left hand of Moses, and Moses confided in him freely about his plans and afterthoughts" (304). Whether or not they had produced Moses was incidental. That Moses's mission was to lead them made them special. That Jethro and God thought Moses competent enough to handle the job made him special. The Israelites, Jethro, and Moses were all clearly God's chosen people. That made them all very special.

IV *Hebrews and American Blacks*

What Hurston has done with the biblical story of Moses is

unique and purposeful. The parallels of the legend with slavery in America are obvious. Both the slaves of Egypt and the slaves of America were unfortunate, oppressed, and exploited. Both came to see themselves as God's chosen people. Blacks in America had recognized and used, in song and story, the analogy between the enslaved Hebrews and the enslaved blacks. It was not uncommon to hear the groans of the enslaved blacks rising from the hot, blistering cotton fields in words that arose from the biblical story:

> Go down, Moses, way down in Egypt's land,
> Tell ole Pharaoh, to let my people go.

Like black slave women, Hebrew women also tried to hide and protect their children from the oppressor. They knew that a cry in the night "might force upon them a thousand years of suffering," that their children could be taken away from them without a moment's notice. Pharaoh, of course, came to be identified with any unfeeling oppressor who profited at the expense of human misery. "Like some antagonists of Afro-Americans," observes Turner, "the Egyptian pharaoh, by deceit and by force, strives to preserve the old order—the slave labor—which his nobles demand."[18] Pharaoh is afraid to do otherwise because to do so would jeopardize his position of power. The nobles, on the other hand, with wisdom reminiscent of the mentality of some slave holders in the antebellum South, see nothing wrong with slavery: "What would slaves want to be free for anyway? They are being fed and taken care of. What more could they want?" (183). Both Pharaoh and the nobles see ruin in social change and thus seek to maintain the status quo.

Moses, in contrast to Pharaoh, becomes a synonym for any deliverer, any honest and hard-working soul who seeks to free the enslaved and guarantee his right to equality and justice. Here, then, as in most of her works, Hurston universalizes her themes. As Blyden Jackson asserts,

art of this kind really fills to the brim the cup of Miss Hurston's desire that a Negro folk experience of life be seen as what it substantially is, the reliable counterpart of every other human being's experience of the same life.[19]

One striking quality of the book is the Civil Rights Movement/ political rhetoric. Moses, who balks the status quo, is called a "radical. He would have the common people talking about equality." The Hebrews circulate a petition in order to express their wishes to Pharaoh. When Moses comes with his plagues and threatens order, the palace priests recommend that Pharaoh "give him some sort of office to keep him quiet" (191). Next they consider bribery. Out in the Wilderness of Sin, the Hebrews "talk about splitting off. Some of them done formed a committee." This committee becomes "the complaint committee" and mediates between Moses and the people. These qualities and similar ones contribute to the Afro-Americanization, or simply the Americanization, of the Biblical Hebrew Movement.

V   A Great Leader

Although Hurston couples folklore and voodoo with a great spiritual experience, the overall tone is poetic and majestic, suggesting the real need of a forceful leader with unusual powers by any enslaved or oppressed people struggling to retain their humanity, their lives. Here, as in her autobiography, Hurston seems to feel that force is necessary to any kind of successful liberation, even in a religious context. For people, no matter who they are, will constantly strive to keep their leaders, as well as each other, down. In *Dust Tracks on a Road*, for instance, she speaks of the Emperor Constantine:

We see the Emperor Constantine, as pagan as he could lay in his hide, having his famous vision of the cross with the injunction: "*In Hoc Signo Vinces*," and arising next day not only to win a great battle but to start out on his missionary journey with his sword. He could not sing like Peter, and he could not preach like Paul. He probably did not even have a good straining voice like my father to win converts and influence people. But he had his good points—one of them being a sword—and a seasoned army. (283–84)

Indeed, says Hurston, "Constantine took up with force where [the Apostle] Paul left off with persuasion" (285). Being a leader, then, is not an easy task, but, as Hurston shows in *Moses, Man of the Mountain*, with patience, perseverance, and force, one can succeed. Moses does not have a sword like Constantine, but he has something better—hoodoo, the budding stick changed to a serpent, water turned to blood, plagues upon Egypt, leprosy upon Miriam, death upon Aaron. The difference between Moses, who is a true leader, and Pharaoh and Aaron who are false and petty, is that Moses is a MAN.[20] And a *man*, of course, in Hurston's world, will always triumph over those who are less than men. Moses, however, is the ultimate man, the absolute man. Though he is a composite of John Buddy of *Jonah's Gourd Vine* and Tea Cake of *Their Eyes Were Watching God*, he is greater than either because he has greater qualities than both:

He is the preacher who meets his adversaries victoriously while John Buddy fails due to character weakness. Moses is the "aristocratic" (beyond monetary concerns) free liver like Tea Cake who knows where true values are to be found, but goes beyond his relationship with Zipporah to one with God while Tea Cake dies having only attained the human sexual plateau. Moses has more and greater stages to experience than John Buddy or Tea Cake, but, of course, his milieu is cosmic.[21]

Irony still lies in the fact, however, that one cannot "lead" another to freedom. The book almost suggests that it is presumptuous to try. Moses is dissatisfied because he hasn't accomplished all that he had hoped. His task was impossible from the beginning, however; one must free one's self.

When he reached the Promised Land, Moses's mission was over. The way hadn't been easy, however; he had learned many painful lessons and settled for much less than he anticipated:

His dreams had in no way been completely fulfilled. He had meant to make a perfect people, free and just, noble and strong, that should be a light for all the world and for time and eternity. And he wasn't sure he had succeeded. He had found out that no man may make another free. Freedom was something internal. The outside signs were just signs and symbols of the man inside. All you could do was to give the opportunity for freedom and the man himself must make his own emancipation. (344–45)

He was able to profit from his mistakes and pass his knowledge on to another great leader, Joshua:

Now one thing I want you to get in your head: You can't have a state of individuals. Everybody just can't be allowed to do as they please. I love liberty and I love freedom so I started off giving everybody a loose rein. But I soon found out that it wouldn't do. A great state is a well-blended mash of something of all the people and all of none of the people. You understand. The liquor of statecraft is distilled from the mash you got. How can a nation speak with one voice if they are not one? Don't forget, now. If you do, you encourage all the stupid but greedy and ambitious to sprout like toadstools and that's the end of right and reason in the state. Coddling and wheedling is not going to stop these destroyers. To a haughty belly, kindness is hard to swallow and harder to digest. (340)

After doing all he could for the Israelites, Moses, in a scene taken from the earlier "Fire and Cloud," climbed Mount Nebo "and headed back over the years" (351). He had done his job and lived his life. Now, like Janie, of *Their Eyes Were Watching God*, all he had left were his memories. As the book closes, he is in search of them:

He stood in the bosom of thunder and the zig-zag lightning above him joined the muttering thunder. Fire and flame played all over the peak where the people could see. The voice of the thunder leaped from peak to plain and Moses stood in the midst of it and said "Farewell." Then he turned with a firm tread and descended the other side of the mountain and headed back over the years. (351)

To the Hebrews, it looks as if Moses died on the mountain; the Bible makes this explicit. By disappearing when and as he does, Moses retains that shroud of mystery which has surrounded him throughout the trip to the Promised Land. It is paramount that he retain that mystery because it has been the only thing that has kept the Hebrews in line; otherwise, they would have killed him before they crossed the Red Sea. This way, Moses is not merely a man to them, but is also a supreme and mysterious being who cannot be totally known by human faculties. In Moses, Hurston gives the old legend new life, infusing it with a universality and appeal hitherto unknown to the Christian world.

Because *Moses, Man of the Mountain* does contain a folk hero who is not prosaic (i.e., does not extol money and materialism), as well as a folk idiom, it is not surprising to find it among

Hurston's works. Just as Hurston felt that there were certain qualities necessary for the ideal man, so she felt certain qualities necessary for the ideal leader. John Buddy fails, in *Jonah's Gourd Vine*, because he is weaker than the community he attempts to lead. Moses, however, after a few stumbles, succeeds handsomely because he realizes, and has at his disposal, those things necessary for effective leadership—force (hoodoo, in this case), respect, consistency, mystery, poetry, and determination. Although he is certainly the Biblical hero responsible for leading the Hebrews out of Egypt, he is also the African hero, Moses, the greatest hoodoo man in the world. Therein lies his importance for Hurston and Africa, and therein lies his importance for the reader of *Moses, Man of the Mountain*.

Moses, Man of the Mountain is a strange amalgam, but an interesting one. Hurston had explored the rich possibilities of biblical sagas in "Fire and Cloud," and *The First One*, and would return to the biblical milieu later for "The Seventh Veil," "The Woman in Gaul," and *Herod the Great* (all unpublished).

VI   "A Noble Failure?"

Finally, however, the book falls short of its mark. On October 4, 1939, Lippincott had written to Carl Van Vechten thanking him for his recommendation of Zora's *Moses, Man of the Mountain* and adding: "It confirms our opinion that this is a remarkable book, possibly a great book."[22] Though many reviewers liked it, Alain Locke called it "caricature instead of portraiture,"[23] and Ralph Ellison said in *New Masses* that "this work sets out to do for Moses what 'The Green Pastures' did for Jehovah; for Negro fiction it did nothing."[24] Hurston, writing to a friend, Edwin Grover, to whom she dedicated the book, admitted, "I have the feeling of disappointment about it. I don't think that I achieved all that I set out to do. I thought that in this book I would achieve my ideal, but it seems that I have not yet reached it. . . . it still doesn't say all that I want it to say."[25] Exactly what "all" Hurston wanted *Moses, Man of the Mountain* to say we will never know. What it does say, however, is ambitious, humorous, and very often noble.

CHAPTER 7

Seraph on the Suwanee

APPEARING on October 11, 1948, *Seraph on the Suwanee*[1] was Hurston's last published novel. It was variously called *Angel in the Bed, Sang the Suwanee in the Spring, The Seraph's Man, Good Morning Sun,* and *Sign of the Sun* before Zora settled on *Seraph on the Suwanee.* Because this novel deals with whites instead of the usual black folks, it has led to charges of assimilationism against Hurston. Perhaps, as some critics have suggested, she was following a new trend among black writers like Willard Motley, Chester Himes, and Ann Petry, who avoided concentrating on black characters. She had written to her editor at Scribner's that "it was 'very much by design' that the book had primarily white characters,"[2] and to Carl Van Vechten on November 2, 1942, that "I have hopes of breaking that old silly rule about Negroes not writing about white people. . . . I am working on the story now."[3] That "story" was *Seraph on the Suwanee.* As Hemenway has noted, however, "The peril in deliberately choosing a white subject is considerable. There is nothing which prohibits a black writer from creating successful white characters, and black literature is full of brilliant white portraits. But if the novelist consciously seeks to portray whites in order to validate his talent, to prove to the world there are no limits to his genius, the very assumptions of the decision become self-defeating."[4] Whether *Seraph on the Suwanee* is self-defeating is debatable, but whatever Hurston's reasons for writing *Seraph on the Suwanee,* to her readers she seemed to be turning traitor, deserting the colorful black folks with whom she had hitherto aligned herself.

Robert Bone dismissed the novel as an assimilationist work which was "written less forcibly than *Their Eyes Were Watching God*"[5] while Darwin Turner explained it as "a conscious adjust-

133

ment to the tastes of a new generation of readers"[6]—readers, pre-
sumably, who would no longer tolerate blacks as fictional characters. What these critics have ignored, however, is the fact that
Hurston never leaves the folk milieu in *Seraph on the Suwanee*.
She does change the color of her characters but she does not
change her themes or environment in any significant way. Although Arvay Henson, the novel's heroine, is white, she, like all
Hurston protagonists, searches for self-actualization and love,
for life-affirming rather than life-denying experiences. White
folks, Hurston perceptively realized, must want those things, too.

As early as *Jonah's Gourd Vine* (1934) Hurston had paved
the way for such a novel as *Seraph on the Suwanee*. By insisting
upon writing her story about "a man" instead of one about the
"traditional lay figures" found in protest fiction about the "Negro
Problem," Hurston was practicing her philosophy that "Human
beings react pretty much the same to the same stimuli. Different
idioms, yes, circumstances and conditions having power to influence, yes. Inherent differences, no." She was interested in
causal analysis, in "what makes a man or a woman do such-and-
so, regardless of his color." In *Seraph on the Suwanee* we have an
individual whose reasons for doing "such-and-so" have little to
do with the color of her skin and everything to do with the state
of her mind, a poor image of self, and a chauvinistic, though extremely loving, husband. In fact, Hurston had written to Burroughs Mitchell, at Scribner's, that she had endowed Arvay with
feelings that she herself had once felt: "Though brash enough
otherwise, I got an overwhelming complex about my looks before I was grown, and it was very hard for a long time for me to
believe that any man really cared for me. I set out to win my
fight against this feeling, and I did."[7]

Although the main characters are white and the style not as
lively or humorous as is typical in Hurston, *Seraph on the Suwanee*'s subject matter differs little from that of Hurston's other
novels. As in most of the other works, including the short stories,
the marriage relationship, the search for true love, and the
growth of the individual are the main focus. Like Hurston's best
novel, *Their Eyes Were Watching God*, *Seraph on the Suwanee*
explores at some length the feminine psyche. Whereas Janie
Crawford is in conflict with the traditions and mores of the so-

ciety in which she lives, however, Arvay Henson is in conflict
with herself. Though she genuinely desires love and happiness,
like Emmaline of the play *Color Struck*, she does everything in
her power to make that love and happiness impossible. She
must end this life-denying battle by learning to appreciate and
respect her worth as a human being. By the time the novel ends,
she has emerged the victor. Having found a comfortable, nurturing spot for herself, she lives.

Other similarities between the two novels are also apparent.
The relationship between Arvay and Jim Meserve, her husband,
as between Janie and Tea Cake, is tender and strong, sexual and
alive. Like Janie, Arvay, who is also a member of the lower class
of southern society, seeks love. And, again like Janie, she almost
misses true love by adhering to the old, traditional way of life.
In this case, Arvay feels bound to her folks who are, in a sense,
tradition. Like Tea Cake, Jim courts boldly and charmingly,
offering a vitally different life from that to which Arvay had
been accustomed. Like both Jody Starks (Janie's second husband) and Tea Cake, Jim devotes himself to providing comfort
for his mate, though his philosophy is not always the *carpe diem*
one of Tea Cake. Like Jody Starks, Jim continuously seeks bigger
and better business ventures.

Seraph on the Suwanee takes place near the turn of this century
in various parts of Florida, and unfolds the complex story of
Arvay Henson Meserve, a poor white woman of Sawley. At sixteen Arvay renounces the world to become a missionary because her sister Larraine marries the man with whom Arvay
imagines herself to be in love. Arvay sees the marriage as an
omen that nothing good will ever happen to her. To compound
her unhappiness she fantasizes about an adulterous relationship
with her sister's husband, and experiences guilt that manifests
itself in the form of body spasms. These fits, sometimes real,
sometimes simulated, keep all potential suitors at a distance
until the manly Jim Meserve arrives in town. By that time,
Arvay is twenty-one.

Jim Meserve is a high-class, rakish Irishman who subdues,
seduces, and marries Arvay, and takes her away from Sawley to
Citrabelle. Though their marriage is occasionally happy, Arvay's
feelings of inferiority and self-pity constantly gnaw at the rela-

tionship until Jim leaves her to find herself and seek him out. Arvay does so but only after shaking off the shackles of the past and embracing what she considers to be her true role—mothering and serving. The bulk of the book is about Arvay's graillike quest for self-actualization. Her task is the more difficult because for over twenty years she belittles herself while simultaneously extolling her folks and the backwoods; she lacks the basic understanding and communicative ability necessary to a good marriage, and seeks shelter from the world rather than active involvement in it.

I *"A Cracker Bred, a Cracker Born"*

Arvay Henson Meserve is a woman who does not think much of herself. This point is brought painfully home so often in the book that the reader gets as sick of the whining heroine as Hurston got when she wrote the novel.[8] At sixteen she believes that "happiness, love and normal relationships were not meant for her. Somehow, God had denied her the fate of sharing in the common happiness and joys of the world." (9). Even when the manly and highly sought-after Jim Meserve expresses an interest in her, Arvay believes herself undeserving: "Ah, no, this pretty, laughing fellow was too far out of her reach. Things as wonderful as this were never meant for nobody like her. This was first-class, and she was born to take other people's leavings" (22). She idolizes Jim in direct proportion to her beratement of self. When Jim mentions marriage, "Arvay began to believe a little in Jim's sincerity. . . . Then a terrible feeling of guilt came over her. Even if Jim meant it, she was not fitten. Here was the most wonderful man in all the world pomping her all up, and she had been living in mental adultery with her sister's husband for all of those wasted years. She was not fitten for a fine man like Jim. He was worth more than she was able to give him" (31–32). Several years into the marriage she still hopes that she might "come to win this great and perfect man some day" (101).

Arvay is so preoccupied with her "adultery of the mind" that she sees the deformity of Earl, her first child, as "punishment for the way I used to be. I thought that I had done paid off, but I reckon not. I never thought it would come like this, but it must be the chastisement I been looking for" (62). She completely ignores the fact that Earl's condition is hereditary—from her father's side of the family. She must heap the blame for everything upon herself.

Because she thinks so little of herself, Arvay thinks extraordinarily high of Jim Meserve. Not only is he a "perfect man" to her, but often she attributes God-like qualities to him. When Jim first expresses his intentions to marry Arvay, for instance, she thinks:

But this was like coming through religion. . . . Like your thoughts while you were out at the praying-ground in the depths of the woods, or being down at the mourners'-bench during protracted meetings with the preacher, deacons and all the folks from the Amen corner standing around and over you begging and pleading with you to turn loose your doubting and only believe. Put your whole faith in the mercy of God and believe. Eternal life, Heaven and its immortal glory were yours if you only would believe. (24)

Later, when a posse seeks to destroy Earl, who has gone berserk, the narrator explains Arvay's opinion of Jim:

But for too many years Arvay had thought of her husband as a being stronger than all others on earth. What God neglected, Jim Meserve took care of. Between the two, God and Jim, all things came to pass. They had charge of things. She had been praying ever since she had found out that Earl was surrounded in that swamp. So far God had not made a move so it was up to Jim. So now, Arvay went to her husband and hung by her arms around his neck as she sank to her knees beside his chair. (133)

Clearly she is about to offer a prayer to this, her second and perhaps greater, god. Even Jim's kiss on her lips "came as a great mercy and a blessing, and Arvay departed from herself and knew nothing until she came to earth again and found herself in the familiar bed" (137). When she reminisces about the twenty years of marriage with Jim, she recalls that "she had stood for moments on the right hand side of God" (153) and that "the most ordinary minute of peace with Jim in the past appeared like time spent in Paradise" (190).

After realizing that most of the people whom she had envied and looked up to actually envied and looked up to her, Arvay comes to accept that though she was a "Cracker bred and a Cracker born," when she died, there did not have to be merely a "Cracker gone." She had the potential for infinitely more than that.

II "See Ten Things and Understand None"

At one point in the novel, Jim excuses Arvay's shortcomings by repeating what Jody Starks says of women in *Their Eyes Were Watching God*—that men see one thing and understand ten while women "see ten things and can't even understand one" (229). Such an opinion is chauvinistic and unflattering to women everywhere, but Arvay's consistent actions are a poor defense against the charge. Not only must most things be explained to her, but they often must be explained without her seeking an explanation or even knowing that she should. Jim compares her to "an unthankful and unknowing hog under a [*sic*] acorn tree. Eating and grunting with your ears hanging over your eyes, and never even looking up to see where the acorns are coming from" (230). The evidence in favor of Jim's simile is overwhelming and begins to blatantly accumulate when Jim moves his family to Citrabelle, Florida.

In Citrabelle, Arvay only looks at the surface of things and concludes accordingly. She sees the fruit-pickers as "sinfully" living on a flowery bed of ease:

Things had a picnicky, pleasury look that, while it was pretty, made Arvay wonder if folks were not taking things too easy down in here. Heaven wasn't going to be any refreshment to folks if they got along with no more trouble than this. . . . It was the duty of man to suffer in this world, and these people round down here in south Florida were plainly shirking their duty. They were living entirely too easy. (64–65)

While Arvay is looking at and judging by appearances, the narrator points out the realities: "She did not know that fruit-cutters seldom worked at all from the end of the season early in June until it opened around the middle of September when they began to cut grapefruit, however short of money they might be" (66). Nor did she know about "the desperate struggle Jim was going through for their very existence" (65). When Jim learns something about citrus-fruit production, acquires a crew, augments the number of boxes the crew cuts by encouraging competition among them, and receives a Christmas turkey as a token of appreciation from the packinghouse manager, "Arvay baked it, and they ate it, but she never asked for the story behind it" (67). That the Meserve couple is at odds is made apparent by the narrator's observations:

Who shall ascend into the hill of the Lord? And who shall stand in His holy place? Arvay thought that it would be herself when and if she could birth Jim a perfect child and by this means tie him forever to her. Jim felt that he would stand on the mount of transfiguration when Arvay showed some appreciation of his love as expressed by what he was striving to do for her. Thus they fumbled and searched for each other in silent darkness. . . . Arvay just had no idea. She had no understanding to what extent she was benefiting from the good will that Jim had been building up ever since he had come to town. She knew nothing of his twisting and turning and conniving to make life pleasant for her sake. . . . She never asked anything, and so Jim never volunteered to tell her. (68–74)

Perhaps what best epitomizes Arvay's "deficiencies" is what happens when she is in her third pregnancy. When Jim learns of the pregnancy he playfully tells Arvay, "You can have that baby, providing that you swear and promise me to bring it here a boy" (85). Though Jim believes that "anybody at all would see through a joke like that. Anybody with even a teaspoonful of sense knows that you can't tell what a child'll turn out to be until it gets born" (92), Arvay spends several painful months "muttering prayers for deliverance from her fancied danger" and caressing her stomach in a plea with the unborn child to "be nice, now, and come here a boy-child for your mama. You see the fix I'm in. Jim is liable to leave me if you ain't a boy" (88). Jim is understating when he says, "There was not sufficient understanding in his marriage" (92).

The climax comes when Jim, ever trying to please and solicit

praise and appreciation from Arvay, foolishly pits his strength
against that of a rattlesnake. He loses the battle and almost
loses his life. Because Arvay can only stand and gawk when
action is required, Jim decides to leave her. As he explains it,

"I feel and believe that you do love me, Arvay, but I don't want
that stand-still, haphazard kind of love. I'm just as hungry as a dog
for a knowing and a doing love. You love like a coward. Don't take
no steps at all. Just stand around and hope for things to happen out
right.

"Your kind of love, Arvay, don't seem to be the right thing for
me. . . . I'm sick and tired of hauling and dragging you along. I'm
tired of excusing you because you don't understand. I'm tired of
waiting for you to meet me on some high place and locking arms
with me and going my way. I'm tired of hunting you, and trying to
free your soul. I'm tired. . . . I'm pushing fifty now, Arvay, and no
use in me hoping no more. I ever loved married life, but since I've
missed it so far, no use in me hoping no further. . . . Oh, we got the
proper papers all right, and without a doubt, the folks around the
court-house are more than satisfied. But to come right down to the
fact of the matter, you and me have never been really married. Our
bonds have never been consecrated. Two people ain't never married
until they come to the same point of view. That we don't seem to be
able to do, so I'm moving over to the coast tomorrow for good."
(230–34)

Arvay must take the first step toward reconciliation. Before she
can do that, however, she must become more communicative,
more understanding. The key is back in Sawley.

III   *Tradition*

The town of Sawley, its traditions, and Arvay's perception of
them are the trouble with Arvay and her marriage. Though
Arvay has always seen herself as a "Cracker," she is secretly
proud of her heritage and considers it a vantage point from which
to look down upon others, mainly blacks, foreigners, and North-
erners. She stubbornly clings to the old ways and allows them
to wreak havoc with her life. She often retreats to the Bible for
answers—a carryover from her teenage days, since the narrator

records no instance of Arvay even attending church after she marries Jim—and dismisses problems as merely in God's plans for her. She must break with her past before she can live her life.

Arvay returns to Sawley when she learns that her mother is terminally ill. The telegram which brings the message seems like a Godsend to her:

God worked in mysterious ways His wonders to perform. . . . God was taking a hand in her troubles. He was directing her ways. The answer was plain. He meant for her to go back home. This was His way of showing her what to do. The Bible said, "Everything after its own kind," and her kind was up there in the piney woods around Sawley. Her family, and the folks she used to know before she fooled herself and linked up with a man who was not her kind. Arvay tossed her head defiantly and rhymed out that she was a Cracker bred and a Cracker born, and when she was dead there'd be a Cracker gone.

As the narrator indicates, however, Arvay is misinterpreting things again:

Arvay was conscious at that moment that she had not really been trying to find the answer that Jim expected of her. As always, she had been trying to defend her background and justify it so that Jim could accept it and her along with it. She had been on the defensive ever since her marriage. The corroding poverty of her childhood became a growing virtue, and a state to be desired. Arvay scorned off learning as a source of evil knowledge and thought fondly of ignorance as the foundation of good-heartedness and honesty. Peace, contentment and virtue hung like a rainbow over turpentine shacks and shanties. . . . Arvay felt eager to get back in the atmosphere of her humble beginnings. (238–39)

When she reaches Sawley, Arvay at first stubbornly clings to the old ways of seeing things. She is distraught to learn that even Sawley has changed: turpentining has been replaced by peanut crops; there are new paved highways, hotels, restaurants, and taxis, none of which, one taxi driver tells Arvay, "the old fogies and dumb peckerwoods" like. Arvay, however, "took sides with the peckerwoods in a timid way." When she expresses her opinion that "in the good old days, the folks in Sawley was good and kind and neighborly," the cab driver belligerently differs:

"Lady! You must not know this town too good. I moved in here fifteen years ago and I done summered and wintered with these folks. I hauled the mud to make some of 'em, and know 'em inside and out. I ain't seen no more goodness and kind-heartedness here than nowhere else. Such another back-biting and carrying on you never seen. They hate like sin to take a forward step. Just like they was took out their cradles, they'll be screwed down in their coffins." (240)

When the taxi drops Arvay at the old Henson place she finds appalling corroborative evidence of the driver's statements. The house is dilapidated; her sister Larraine, whom she had envied years before, is "in a ton of coarse-looking flesh, a cheap cotton dress and dirty white cotton stockings"; her brother-in-law Carl, for whom she had renounced the world when she was sixteen, is now clearly "soiled", "heavy-set," "drab," "marred," "chuckle-headed"—"But for 'Raines intervention, she might have been married to Carl. Been the mother of those awful-looking young men and women that he had fathered. Had to get in bed with something like that! Do Jesus!" (254). Arvay begins to renounce the house, the people, their lives.

Larraine and Carl behave so niggardly that it is easy for Arvay to turn her back on them. The house, however, must be burned because it stands between her mulberry tree, beneath which "her real life had begun" (268), and the world. It epitomizes and symbolizes her stifled life:

Seeing it from the meaning of the tree it was no house at all. It was an evil, ill-deformed monstropolous accumulation of time and scum. It had soaked in so much of doing-without, of soul-starvation, of brutish vacancy of aim, of absent dreams, envy of trifles, ambitions for littleness, smothered cries and trampled love, that it was a sanctuary of tiny and sanctioned vices. Its walls were smoked over with the vapors from dead souls like smokey kerosene lamps. . . . The house had caught a distemper from the people who had lived in it, and had then diseased up people. No, it was no longer just a building. It had caught a soul of its own now. It caught people and twisted the limbs of their minds. . . . How much had it blinded her from seeing and feeling through the years! (269)

After burning the house, Arvay "had made a peace and was in harmony with her life." She has come to the same viewpoint as her husband. Nothing remains but to seek him out and belatedly begin her marriage.

IV *"The Morning" of Arvay's Life*

After the timely revelations back in Sawley, Arvay concludes that "Certainly the afternoon of her life was more pleasant than the morning had been" (262). The "morning" had been so unpleasant because it had been full of shelters and havens, all escapes from the realities of life. Even her decision to become a missionary was an attempt to retire from the world.

When Jim first meets Arvay he responds to her pleas to leave her alone with "You need my help and my protection too bad for that. . . . I have to stay with you and stand by you and give my protection to keep you from hurting your ownself too much" (15). Arvay comes to believe him and has "a tremulous desire to take refuge in this man. To be forever warm and included in the atmosphere that he stirred up around him" (22). Jim throws his "strong arm of protection" around her, all to no avail. He cannot free her soul. Only Arvay can do that. As Moses learns in *Moses, Man of the Mountain,* one individual may not make another free. One must do that for himself. By destroying her shackling past, Arvay breaks free and is finally ready to embrace life. Significantly, this is only made possible when Jim removes his "strong arm of protection." Unsheltered, unprotected, Arvay tackles her past and wins. She is self-sufficient, an individual in her own right. She can now protect Jim, "prop him up on every leaning side." By the end of the novel, the trend has been ironically reversed. Arvay is now hovering Jim: "Inside he was nothing but a little boy to take care of, and he hungered for her hovering. Look at him now! Snuggled down and clutching onto her like Kenny when he wore diapers. Arvay felt such a swelling to protect and comfort Jim that tears came up in her eyes. So helpless sleeping there in her arms and trusting himself to her" (310).

V *Chauvinism*

Unflattering attitudes about women occupy a more prominent position in this novel than in any of the other Hurston works. The view that Hurston has her characters present is the traditional male one, and shows that women have been regarded as brainless, thoughtless, inferior, helpless wretches for many, many years. Early in the novel, Jim rather authoritatively declares that

women folks don't have no mind to make up nohow. They wasn't made for that. Lady folks were just made to laugh and act loving and kind and have a good man to do for them all he's able, and have him as many boy-children as he figgers he'd like to have, and make him so happy that he's willing to work and fetch in every dad-blamed thing that his wife thinks she would like to have. That's what women are made for. (23)

Believing that "a woman knows who her master is" (31), Jim continues to verbalize his opinions throughout the novel. Before her marriage, Arvay correctly interprets his meaning:

He had just as good as excused the woman he married from all worry and bother. In so many words he had said, "Love and marry me and sleep with me. That is all I need you for. Your brains are not sufficient to help me with my work; you can't think with me. Putting your head on the same pillow with mine is not the same thing as mingling your brains with mine anymore than crying when I cry is giving you the power to feel my sorrow. You can feel my sympathy but not my sorrow." All in all, that meant that if she married Jim Meserve, her whole duty as a wife was to just love him good, be nice and kind around the house and have children for him. (32–33)

Jim obviously feels that women are to be subjugated to the will and whim of men. Once when Arvay is particularly irritating, for instance, he orders her to strip. When she tries to cover herself, Jim responds with: "Don't you move! You're my damn property, and I want you right where you are, and I want you naked. Stand right there in your tracks until I tell you that you can move" (190). When Jim finally "allows" Arvay to get in bed, he "stretched himself full length upon her, but in the same way that he might have laid himself down on a couch" (190).

Even Joe Kelsey, an oppressed minority himself, believes women to be property. When Jim tells of his difficulty understanding Arvay, Joe advises: "Make 'em knuckle under. From the very first jump, get the bridle in they mouth and ride 'em hard and stop 'em short. Theys all alike, boss. Take 'em and break 'em" (41). Joe's advice is very much like Killicks's practice with Janie in *Their Eyes Were Watching God*: Janie's grandmother is right, then, in believing that some men will treat a woman like a spit cup.

When Arvay worries herself sick in fear of giving birth to a girl when Jim has expressed a firm desire to have a boy, Jim excuses her and blames it on her sex:

Arvay had acted dumb, but what more could you expect? She was a woman and women folks were not given to thinking nohow. It was not in their make-up to do much thinking. That was what men were made for. Women were made to hover and to feel. (93)

Jim Meserve, then, is a chauvinist who believes that a woman's role is to mother and to serve. Even his name—"Me-serve"—emphasizes his attitude. On the other hand, however, Jim's name can mean "Me serve you." Certainly he does serve Arvay, and it soon becomes apparent to everyone but Arvay that he wants more from her than just "loving him good, being nice and kind around the house and having children for him." His name, then, like his attitude, is often ambivalent. Too, Jim seems to need a mother and looks to Arvay to fulfill that need:

There was something about Arvay that put him in mind of his mother. They didn't favor each other in the face, but there was something there that was the same. Maybe that was what had caught his attention the first time that he had laid eyes on Arvay. Maybe that was why he had never missed his family since he married her. All the agony of his lost mother was gone when he could rest his head on Arvay's bosom and go to sleep at nights. (94)

As far as Jim is concerned, his marriage to Arvay will never be a real one until she sees things as he does. By the end of the novel, their views are the same because Arvay has come to accept

her role as mother. When Jim snuggles up to her in the last
scene in the novel, she realizes that

her job was mothering. What more could any woman want and
need?. . . . Jim was hers and it was her privilege to serve him. To keep
on like that in happiness and peace until they died together giving
Jim the hovering that he needed. (310–11)

Whether Arvay makes the right decision here is questionable.
She has, after all, consciously chosen to mother and serve. And
as Robert Hemenway laments, "Just as Arvay begins to become
interesting, she is lost again to domestic service."[9] Perhaps the
important thing here, however, is that, for the first time in her
life, Arvay has found a place for herself and is totally happy.
Jim is happy and their relationship seems complete. Perhaps,
then, whatever makes both of them happy and content is the
right decision. Too, because Arvay now appreciates her own
worth, and has elected a spot that will be nurturing and fulfilling,
her potential for growth is greatly increased.

Where Hurston stands on all this is unclear. At times she does
seem distantly ironic when she has Arvay ask, "What more could
a woman want?" Too, when this novel is compared with *Their
Eyes Were Watching God*, contradictions are noticeable. Janie
Starks, for instance, chooses not to serve Killicks and Starks, not
to conform to their ideas of the subservient role of woman. Perhaps Arvay's decision to serve in *Seraph on the Suwanee* illustrates Hurston's belief that people are individuals—that is, what
is right for one is not necessarily right for another. To Hurston,
the happiness of the individual is paramount. And, undeniably,
Arvay Henson is happy. By contrast, Zora Hurston was never able
to put love, mothering or serving before her own career. Though
she was married at least twice and involved in a number of love
affairs, she always returned, sometimes even escaped, to her
career.

The omission of folktales (though some familiar—familiar
mostly because of the other Hurston works—folk sayings and
metaphors are included) makes *Seraph on the Suwanee* an
anomaly among Hurston's works. She was obviously moving in
a more somber and complex direction in this novel. The lan-

guage and style are controlled as the reader is given an un-relieved, in-depth view into the mind of a sick woman. No comic relief is forthcoming in this novel; no deceptively simple, en-gaging style is apparent. The language no longer flows along smoothly and naturally. Rather, it moves slowly and must be read slowly. It is not poetic, as Hurston's language generally is, but is, instead, what Robert Bone would call prosaic and "causes many readers to yearn for the alleviating farce and carefree gaiety of the earlier works."[10]

Perhaps Hurston was consciously aligning her style with the kind of story she was relating. Arvay Henson, after all, is a character completely without a sense of humor. And, although narrated in the third person, almost everything in the story is filtered through her consciousness. What style is more appropri-ate, then, than one which is as somber as the heroine whose story it relates? Too, the style seems appropriate because Hurston seemed to see whites as being more somber, more materialistic, more prosaic, and thus less unrelieved (see the chapter on *Their Eyes Were Watching God*) than blacks. Whereas Janie Starks can laugh and play as well as cry and work, Arvay Henson seems incapable of such a gamut of emotions. And whereas Janie and Tea Cake form a real team, Arvay constantly fights Jim because she believes that his playing is sinful.

VI   *Hurston: An Assimilationist?*

Seraph on the Suwanee, then, is a complex and different novel, but it is not necessarily an assimilationist one. It is true that all of the major characters are white, but, as in her other novels, Hurston simply seems to be writing about people, about indi-viduals coming to terms with themselves, regardless of their color. Since Hurston only published one novel about white characters, it is difficult to determine whether she was becoming an assimilationist or whether she was simply writing a novel to exemplify her personal beliefs about people. Had other novels followed the publication of *Seraph on the Suwanee,* it would have been easier to determine the direction in which Hurston was moving. When she died in 1960, however, she was working on a history of Herod the Great, hardly an assimilationist piece.

In her works, Hurston seems to be writing about people who
have been hurt, sometimes by themselves, sometimes by others,
but who must heal themselves, who must realize that the individual has the means to pull himself up. In *Their Eyes Were
Watching God*, it takes Janie almost thirty years; in *Seraph on
the Suwanee*, it takes Arvay at least twenty. But both, one black,
the other white, succeed and are happy. In *Seraph on the
Suwanee*, Hurston appears confident in her medium and in her
ability, though as she told Marjorie Kinnan Rawlings, she was
not particularly pleased with the novel: "I am not so sure that I
have done my best, but I tried. I need not tell you that my goal
eludes me. I am in despair because it keeps ever ahead of me."[11]
Hurston died before she could reach her goal. Her mother had
encouraged her to jump at the stars. She had jumped but had
apparently fallen short of the mark. In her autobiography she
wrote:

I regret all of my books. It is one of the tragedies of life that one
cannot have all the wisdom one is ever to possess in the beginning.
Perhaps, it is just as well to be rash and foolish for a while. If writers
were too wise, perhaps no books would be written at all. It might be
better to ask yourself "Why?" afterwards than before. Anyway, the
force from somewhere in Space which commands you to write in
the first place, gives you no choice. You take up the pen when you
are told, and write what is commanded. There is no agony like bearing
an untold story inside you.[12]

Hurston wrote this at least six years before *Seraph on the
Suwanee* was published. She never gave up the battle, then.
Those stories had to be told. Though her goal might have eluded
her, at least her agony was significantly decreased.

CHAPTER 8

Nonfiction

A MONG Hurston's works are three books of nonfiction: *Mules and Men* (1935),[1] *Tell My Horse* (1938),[2] and *Dust Tracks on a Road* (1942).[3] The first two books are collections of folklore; the third is Hurston's autobiography. All three are personal and engaging, and need to be seriously considered in any study of Hurston's works.

I *Folklore*

Mules and Men combines folktales and hoodoo practices, while *Tell My Horse* is almost exclusively an authoritative text on Hoodoo. Both books resulted from research grants awarded to Hurston to collect folklore among blacks in the United States and the West Indies. Although a few writers, both black and white, had used folklore in their writings, Hurston, along with her contemporary, J. Mason Brewer, led the way in compiling and publishing a significant, substantial collection of folklore.

II Mules and Men

The results of research conducted between 1927 and 1932, *Mules and Men* is by far the more valuable of the two folklore collections. Divided into two distinct parts, the book contains folklore from Florida and Louisiana, as well as an introduction by Franz Boas, illustrations by Miguel Covarrubias, a glossary, and an appendix containing Negro songs with music, formulae of Hoodoo doctors, a list of paraphernalia of conjure, and prescriptions of root doctors.

The book sought a publisher in various forms, though the book's core remained the same, between 1929 and 1934. It did

not find a publisher until after *Jonah's Gourd Vine* had been
accepted by Lippincott. Even then, Zora was asked to revise the
manuscript "so that it would not be too technical for the average
reader," and to extend it so that the publisher, Lippincott, could
have a $3.50 book. To comply, Zora "inserted the between-
story conversation and business," condensed an earlier hoodoo
article, "Hoodoo in America," which had appeared in 1931 in
the *Journal of American Folklore*, and added it as the last third
of the book.[4]

Part I concerns itself with folklore gathered in Florida. Narrated in the first person, this section records Hurston's return
to her native city of Eatonville with its "love of talk and song."
Although Hurston later visits other parts of Florida—Polk County,
for instance—the nature of the tales remains the same. Unfortunately, Hurston makes little effort to classify or analyze the tales,
but merely reports them in the order and manner in which she
hears them. As a result, the subject matter and Hurston as nar-
rator/character are the only things which give the book continuity. The practice of reporting folklore indiscriminately was,
of course, a common practice among folklorists during Hurston's
day. Had Hurston classified her tales, however, some much-
needed order could have been achieved. On the other hand,
perhaps classification would have been tampering with natural
art. It was important to present the raw material unadulterated
by authorial whims and preferences. What we have in *Mules
and Men*, then, is a kind of free association of ideas whereby
one tale naturally leads to another because one tale "reminds"
a listener, who is also a potential teller, of another tale. Often
a second tale is merely an attempt to alleviate or mitigate the
effects of the first tale.

The tales themselves are simple and varied; some, because
they have little point, are told merely for the joy of storytelling.
Others are adaptations of the more traditional Brer Rabbit
stories so popular in the South, tall tales of the lumber camp,
and tales of the black folk hero, John. John, however, is care-
fully distinguished from the mythical John Henry of the white
storytellers. In the glossary, Hurston says of him:

Jack or John (not John Henry) is the great human culture hero in

Negro folk-lore. He is like Daniel in Jewish folk-lore, the wish-fulfillment hero of the race. The one who, nevertheless, or in spite of laughter, usually defeats Ole Massa, God and the Devil. Even when Massa seems to have him in a hopeless dilemma he wins out by a trick. Brer Rabbit, Jack (or John) and the Devil are continuations of the same thing. (305)

John, then, like Moses, is a great folk hero. Although he does not outwit God in any of the tales in *Mules and Men,* he is confident in his ability to outwit white men and the devil. Though, in reality, blacks seldom came out on top, in their tales they invariably triumphed over the white oppressor. The rabbit appears in few tales, but Hurston accounts for this deficiency by explaining that native Floridians tell their stories about the gopher, the equivalent, for them, of the rabbit.

The tales are usually related in "lying sessions," like those held around Joe Clarke's store porch in some of Hurston's other works, as one storyteller tries to outdo the other. One typical session is a contest among lumberjacks to describe an ugly man. One speaker says, "Ah seen a man so ugly till they had to spread a sheet over his head so sleep could slip up on him." Another counters, "Ah'm goin' to talk with my mouth wide open. Those men y'all talkin' 'bout wasn't ugly at all. Those was pretty men. Ah knowed one so ugly till you could throw him in the Mississippi River and skim ugly for six months." Another agrees, "He ain't lying. Ah knowed dat same man. He didn't die—he jus' uglied away" (94).

Many of the tales have distinct characteristics which suggest a kind of formula for storytelling. They often begin and end with lines of native poetry which themselves are rarely, if ever, related to the tales they preface or conclude. Rather, they seem to function as convenient vehicles for getting in and out of tales—much like "Once upon a time" and "they lived happily ever after" do in popular fairy tales. One storyteller, for instance, introduces his tale of a "nigger dat found a gold watch" (115) with, "Well, once upon a time was a good ole time./Monkey chew tobacco and spit white lime" (115), while typical endings range from

> Biddy, biddy, bend my story is end.
> Turn loose de rooster and hold de hen. (132)

> 'Bout dat time a flea wanted to get a
> hair cut, so Ah left. (167)

> Goat fell down and skint his chin
> Great God A'mighty how de goat did grin. (214)

All of the tales, no matter what their import, serve a common purpose—to give an inside view into the often deceptive, highly imaginative character of the Negro. In her introduction, Hurston explains how difficult such a view is to come by:

The Negro, in spite of his open-faced laughter, his seeming acquiescence, is particularly evasive. You see we are a polite people and we do not say to our questioner, "Get out of here!" We smile and tell him or her something that satisfies the white person because, knowing so little about us, he doesn't know what he is missing. The Indian resists curiosity by a stony silence. The Negro offers a feather-bed resistance. That is, we let the probe enter, but it never comes out. It gets smothered under a lot of laughter and pleasantries. (18–19)

Later, Hurston explains how blacks use laughter as disguise: "The brother in black puts a laugh in every vacant place in his mind. His laugh has a hundred meanings. It may mean amusement, anger, grief, bewilderment, chagrin, curiosity, simple pleasure or any other of the known or undefined emotions" (88–89). Because Hurston was herself from a culture similar to those she probed, and because she had the "spy-glass of Anthropology" at her disposal, after a few false starts, she had little trouble making friends and thereby obtaining the material she sought: "Zestful towards her material, and completely unashamed of it, she ingratiated herself with the tellers of tall tales in the turpentine camps, or on store porches, and with the preachers of tall sermons in backwoods churches."[5]

Just as Blacks had their own ideas about the ability of John (or Jack or Brer Rabbit) to outwit everyone else, so they fantasized about how slaves obtained their freedom, and how work came about—"God made de world and de white folks made

work" (101). Interestingly, the tale related to verify this assertion corresponds exactly with Nanny's views, in *Their Eyes Were
Watching God*, on how men treat women:

Know how it happened? After God got thru makin' de world and de
varmints and de folks, he made up a great big bundle and let it
down in de middle of de road. It laid dere for thousands of years,
then Ole Missus said to Ole Massa: "Go pick up dat box, Ah want
to see whut's in it." Ole Massa look at de box and it look so heavy
dat he says to de nigger, "Go fetch me dat big ole box out dere in
de road." De nigger been stumblin' over de box a long time so he
tell his wife:
    "'Oman, go git dat box." So de nigger 'oman she runned to git
de box. She says:
    "Ah always lak to open up a big box 'cause there's nearly always
something good in great big boxes." So she run and grabbed a-hold
of de box and opened it up and it was full of hard work.
    Dat's de reason de sister in black works harder than anybody else
in de world. De white man tells de nigger to work and he takes and
tells his wife. (101–102)

III   *Hoodoo*

In the introduction to Part II of *Mules and Men*, Hurston explains that, although she had enjoyed gathering folktales in
Florida, she had done nothing about Hoodoo. "So I slept a
night, and the next morning I headed my toe-nails toward
Louisiana and New Orleans in particular" (229). The remainder
of the book recounts her experiences with various hoodoo doctors.
As a true anthropologist and folklorist, Hurston wished to experience voodoo rites firsthand. She thus underwent initiation
rites with various hoodoo practitioners, from Eulalia, who specialized in man and woman cases, to Dr. Samuel Jenkins, who
specialized in "reading the cards."
    Although all of the initiation rites are elaborate, the most
extraordinary one takes place at the hands of Luke Turner, a
popular hoodoo doctor in New Orleans. Not only is Hurston
crowned with a consecrated snake skin, but "naked as I came
into the world," she also fasts for sixty-nine hours as "a sort of
going to the wilderness in the spirit" (247). Hurston undergoes

similar, though less elaborate, rites while studying with others, but unfortunately she never relates the results. Rather, perhaps to keep the cult as secret as possible, she drops the matter after reciting the details of several of the prescriptions.

Suprisingly, in her travels through Louisiana Hurston found hoodoo to be widespread:

Hoodoo, or Voodoo, as pronounced by the whites, is burning with a flame in America with all the intensity of a suppressed religion. It has its thousands of secret adherents. It adapts itself like Christianity to its locale, reclaiming some of its borrowed characteristics to itself. Such as fire-worship as signified in the Christian church by the altar and the candles. And the belief in the power of water to sanctify as in baptism. (229)

Explaining that "belief in magic is older than writing" (229), Hurston traces its beginnings to God—"Six days of magic spells and mighty words and the world with its elements above and below was made" (229)—and as *Moses, Man of the Mountain* attests, to Moses himself.

Mules and Men is an interesting and entertaining collection which offers valuable insight into a class of people and a way of life. The folklore recorded here is anticipated in Hurston's short stories and later appears in *Jonah's Gourd Vine* and *Their Eyes Were Watching God,* where people of the community gather around Joe Clarke's (Jody Starks's in *Their Eyes Were Watching God*) porch to trade lies. Although this collection is interesting and entertaining, however, Sterling Brown found it to be idyllic: "There seem to be omissions. The picture is too pastoral, with only a bit of grumbling about hard work, or a few slave anecdotes that turn the tables on old marster. . . ."[6] In an unidentified newspaper clipping dated February 25, 1936, Brown also praises *Mules and Men* but finds that though Hurston's characters "are naive, quaint, complaisant, bad enough to kill each other in jooks," they are

meek otherwise, socially unconscious. Their life is made to appear easy-going and carefree. This makes *Mules and Men* singularly incomplete. These people live in a land shadowed by squalor, poverty, disease, violence, enforced ignorance and exploitation. Even if browbeaten, they do know a smouldering resentment. . . . From the reviewer's own experience, he knows that harsher folktales await the collector. These people brood upon their hardships, talk about them "down by the big-gate," and sometimes even at the big house. They are not blind, and they are not being fooled; some have lost their politeness, and speak right out. *Mules and Men* should be more bitter, it would be nearer the total truth.[7]

This sort of criticism was to plague Hurston for the rest of her career. When Richard Wright reviewed *Their Eyes Were Watching God* in 1937, he was scathing: "Miss Hurston voluntarily continues in her novel the tradition which was *forced* upon the Negro in the theater, that is, the minstrel technique that makes the 'white folks' laugh. Her characters eat and laugh and cry and work and kill; they swing like a pendulum eternally in that safe and narrow orbit in which America likes to see the Negro live: between laughter and tears."[8]

Harold Preece, a white radical, attacked Zora for "devoting her literary abilities to recording the legendary amours of terrapins." According to the omniscient Preece, "when a Negro author describes her race with such a servile term as 'Mules and Men' critical members of the race must necessarily evaluate the author as a literary climber."[9] The omissions can probably be explained if we remember that Hurston sought to capture the sometimes happy, affirmative side of black life, to show that the picture of blacks being "saturated with our sorrows" was a false one: "We talk about the race problem a great deal, but go on living and laughing and striving like everybody else." She felt it "urgent to realize that the minorities do think, and think about something other than the race problem,"[10] that, in spite of the atrocities levied against them, blacks continued to function, to bloom like Alice Walker's petunias, to grow deep like Langston Hughes's river. This very intent was a protest against established, often "impaired" tradition, a tribute to the creative bents of a people.

In spite of its omissions, *Mules and Men* is a valuable addition to any folklore collection. Franz Boas, in his foreword to the book, explains its value:

To the student of cultural history the material presented is valuable not only by giving the Negro's reaction to every day events, to his emotional life, his humor and passions, but it throws into relief also the peculiar amalgamation of African and European tradition which is so important for understanding historically the character of American Negro life, with its strong African background in the West Indies, the importance of which diminishes with increasing distance from the south. (8)

IV   Tell My Horse

Tell My Horse is, unfortunately, not as engaging as *Mules and Men*. Set for the most part in Haiti and the British West Indies, this book records Hurston's experiences with and reactions to the people of those areas. As in *Mules and Men*, however, Hurston reports the unimportant as well as the important, the trivial as well as the significant. As a result, the reader often longs for relief.

The merit of *Tell My Horse* lies mainly in the fact that it reports folklore practices which differ substantially from those practiced in the United States, and thus from those described in *Mules and Men*. In this book, then, we are in a different, sometimes foreign world.

In some essays Hurston discusses Brother Hnansi, the Spider, a culture hero who is personated in Haiti by Ti Malice and in the United States by Brer Rabbit; the fascination with duppies, the most powerful part of any man; people mating with non-human objects (Hurston records one instance, for example, of a man who "had a covenant with a tree on the sunny side"); and the preparation of young Jamaican girls by specialists for marriage. The preparation of young females for marriage manifests the place of woman in a society in which her only function is to afford pleasure to a man who can divorce her simply by returning her to her parents. Of women in the Caribbean (Chapter V) Hurston writes:

Of course all women are inferior to all men by God and law down there. But if a woman is wealthy, of good family and mulatto, she can overcome some of her drawbacks. But if she is of no particular family, poor and black, she is in a bad way indeed in that man's world. She had better pray to the Lord to turn her into a donkey and be done with the thing. It is assumed that God made poor black females for beasts of burden, and nobody is going to interfere with providence. Most assuredly no upper class man is going to demean himself by assisting one of them with a heavy load. If he were caught in such an act he probably would become an outcast among his kind. It is just considered down there that God made two kinds of donkeys, one kind that can talk. The black women of Jamaica load banana boats now, and the black women used to coal ships when they burned coal. (76)

Tell My Horse, however, does much more than discuss folk-lore. The sections on Jamaica and Haiti, for instance, consider the more serious problems of race and politics. Part I, which consists of five essays on Jamaica, centers about problems of color and race. The mulattoes of Jamaica, records Hurston, generally claim percentages, however small, of the white blood of their fathers while completely ignoring the existence of black mothers (Zora thought of writing an article about "this island where roosters lay eggs"):[11]

The color line in Jamaica between the white Englishman and the blacks is not as sharply drawn as between the mulattoes and the blacks. To avoid the consequences of posterity the mulattoes give the blacks a first class letting alone. There is a frantic stampede white-ward to escape from Jamaica's black mass. (16)

Hurston explains the natives' attitude by noting that

under ordinary circumstances the trend would be towards the majority group, of course. But one must remember that Jamaica has slavery in her past and it takes many generations for the slave derivatives to get over their awe for the master-kind. Then there is the colonial attitude. Add to that the Negro's natural aptitude for imitation and you have Jamaica. (16–17)

The solution to the situation, suggests Hurston, is time. After all, "some Americans are still aping the English as best they can even though they have had one hundred and fifty years to recover" (16).

Part II of *Tell My Horse* is a series of essays on the chaotic political and social climate of Haiti. Significantly, this section on Haiti is the first indication of Hurston's profound interest in politics which would consume her life during the years between the publication of her last book in 1948 and her death in 1960. Hurston writes authoritatively of politics though at this point she was barely a novice. Her opinions on the causes of the social upheavals are to be taken as simply that—her opinions, which may or may not have had any basis in fact.

Part III studies Haitian Voodoo. Of its religious base, Hurston says:

In the beginning God and His woman went into the bedroom together to commence creation. That was the beginning of everything and Voodoo is just as old as that. It is the old, old mysticism of the world in African terms. Voodoo is a religion of creation and life. It is the worship of the sun, the water and other natural forces, but the symbolism is no better understood than that of other religions and consequently is taken too literally. (137)

In very explicit terms, Hurston also explains the sexual symbols of voodoo belief—"The uplifted forefinger in greeting in Voodoo is really phallic and that means the male attributes of the Creator. The handclasp that ends in the fingers of one hand encircling the thumb of the other signifies the vulva encircling the penis, denoting the female aspect of deity" (137)—and the widespread belief in, and fear of, zombies—soulless bodies called back from the dead. "No one can stay in Haiti long without hearing Zombies mentioned in one way or another, and the fear of this thing and all that it means seeps over the country like a ground current of cold air. This fear is real and deep. It is more like a group of fears" (189). To give the belief credence, Hurston even photographed a zombie and included its picture in *Tell My Horse.* She had been warned by a government physician that the secret of the zombies might cost her "a great deal to learn. . . . Perhaps it will cost you more than you are willing to pay." Though she was not able to discover "what is the whole truth and nothing else but the truth about Zombies," she was able to say with conviction: "I know that there are Zombies in Haiti."

Hurston reports her findings, however bizarre, both sympathetically and objectively. It may seem to some that she presents the people in a less than flattering light with her broad humor and lowly material. But, as Benjamin Brawley says of Hurston's works, Hurston presents the untutored Negro "without apology, a character as good as other characters but different. Taking a bright story wherever it may be found, she passes it on, leaving to others the duty and pleasure of philosophizing."[12] *Tell My Horse* understandably did not sell well. Not only is it tedious in too many places but it often passes off village gossip and "hear-say" as facts, thereby drawing fire from some anthropologists. A reviewer, Harold Courlander, writing in the *Saturday Review*, sums up the book's virtues and vices: the book is "a curious mixture of remembrance, travelogue, sensationalism and anthropology. The remembrances are vivid, the travelogue tedious, the sensationalism reminiscent of Seabrook and the anthropology a melange of misinterpretation and exceedingly good folklore."[13]

Tell My Horse and *Mules and Men* are both useful works in the field of Voodoo. Hurston's final word on the subject, however, is found in her autobiography, *Dust Tracks on a Road*: "If science ever gets to the bottom of Voodoo in Haiti and Africa, it will be found that some important medical secrets, still unknown to medical science, give it its power rather than the gestures of ceremony" (213).

As a folklorist, Hurston has received considerable attention. James W. Byrd praises her as an important contributor to the American folk tradition: "In recent years, Negro fictionists have joined their white colleagues in showing a growing interest in the rural South, which is rich in the folklore of whites and Negroes. Foremost among these Negro writers is Zora Neale Hurston of Florida."[14] What is most important is that Hurston has accumulated a rich body of cultural expression which has revealed ways of living and ways of thinking hitherto hidden from the white world. She has thus made the public pleasantly aware of the Negro as a contributor to American folk tradition in particular, and to folk tradition in general.

As source material for her novels, the books of folklore are also important. The practice of holding "lying sessions" for the purpose of determining the best liar, for instance, becomes a technique in *Their Eyes Were Watching God* (1937). The characters and the subject matter are essentially the same, offering a kind of comic relief from the drudgeries of mundane existence. Traditionally, the Uncle Remus and Brer Rabbit tales have been attributed to the black race. Because she collected new kinds of folktales which earlier collectors either did not find or tended to ignore, however, Hurston has brought the nonanimal tale to prominence. By collecting all kinds of tales, Hurston has preserved from oblivion much of the lore significant for an insight not only into a people but into a past.

V Dust Tracks on a Road

Just as *Mules and Men* and *Tell My Horse* are significant for the insight they offer into a people and their past, so is *Dust Tracks on a Road* valuable because of the insight it offers into Zora Neale Hurston and her past. In the tradition of Frederick Douglass's *Narrative* and Booker T. Washington's *Up From Slavery*, the book is the American success story—from rags to fleeting riches, anonymity to recognition—a story of individual enterprise and initiative. In his introduction to the book, Darwin Turner says of her: "Zora Neale Hurston the individual is as interesting as Zora Neale Hurston the writer, and an attempt to understand her personality and social attitudes is prerequisite to a study of her fiction."[15] Hurston's autobiography may not be a prerequisite for her fiction (hitherto, it has only muddied the waters), but any study of Hurston and her works is incomplete without it. As Hurston herself says in *Dust Tracks on a Road*: "Like the dead-seeming, cold rocks, I have memories within that come out of the material that went to make me. Time and Place have had their say. So you will have to know something about the time and place where I came from, in order that you may interpret the incidents and directions of my life" (11). But, as Hemenway adds, Hurston's "total career, not her autobiography, is the proof of her achievement and the best index to her life and art. Only when considered in that total context can the book be properly assessed."[16]

Hurston wrote *Dust Tracks on a Road* in California, where she had gone at the invitation of a rich friend, Katharane Edson Mershon, to relax and rest. Instead of resting, however, she worked as a story consultant at Paramount Studios (October 1941–January 1942) and wrote her life story, a story which won the *Saturday Review*'s $1,000 Anisfield Award for its contribution to better race relations. Written only at the urging of her editor and published in late November 1942, the book was meant to be the first volume of a multi-volume work. Understandably, no second volume appeared. Zora "did not want to write it at all, because it is too hard to reveal one's inner self"[17] and after 1942 there were few successes to speak of, even fewer stories she wished to tell.

Dust Tracks on a Road begins with Zora's birth and childhood "as told to her" by others: "This is all hear-say. Maybe some of the details of my birth as told me might be a little inaccurate, but it is pretty well established that I really did get born" (35). Fittingly, Zora's birth does not come until Chapter 3 of the book. Chapters 1 and 2 are devoted, respectively, to "My Birth-place"—the all-black incorporated self-governing town of Eaton-ville, Florida, which Hurston describes as "burly, boiling, hard-hitting, rugged-individualistic"—and "My Folks"—John Hurston, a mulatto from "over the creek" and "dark-brown Lucy Ann Potts of the land-owning Richard Potts." It is only after Zora has thus set the stage, the rich incubator of her own birth, that she makes her entrance. She introduces hereslf as a mystical, imaginative, ambitious, intelligent, combative child in harmony with her environment, but often in disharmony with her father, who wished to curb her ambition. She is very much a part of Eaton-ville and she conveys a sense of community and roots in the early part of the book.

The book itself is a very informal, conversational narrative about the people and places which form the background of Hurston's life. Although Hurston's mother, Lucy Ann Potts, is important, it is her father, John Hurston, who dominates the early part of the book. Perhaps this is because John Hurston, his behavior and activities, had such a profound effect upon his daughter. Not only did he threaten to cut his throat when he heard that he had a second daughter (Sarah was the first), but he also frequently threatened to violently rid Zora of her high and mighty attitude. "Let me change words with him—and I am of the word-changing kind—" says Hurston, "and he was ready to change ends." Because her mother was on her side and took her part frequently, however, Zora managed to escape the wrath of her father. When she was nine,[18] her mother died, leaving her and her siblings at the mercy of John Hurston and the new wife he took within a few weeks of Lucy's death. The new wife, jealous of any attentions John showed his children, persuaded him to banish them all from the house, thereby precipitating an event which obsessed Hurston throughout her life. Not only is the event frequently mentioned in *Dust Tracks on a Road,* but the second marriage itself figures prominently in *Jonah's Gourd Vine* where John Hurston is thinly disguised as John Buddy Pearson and his second wife as Hattie Tyson.

After her mother's death Hurston's life was not easy. Not only was she "passed around like a bad penny" from neighbor to neighbor, but she attended school only sporadically and knew the distinct taste of poverty and unhappiness. The desolation of those years is best described in her own words:

There is something about poverty that smells like death. Dead dreams dropping off the heart like leaves in a dry season and rotting around the feet; impulses smothered too long in the fetid air of underground caves. The soul lives in a sickly air. People can be slave-ships in shoes. (124)

Zora persevered, however, and as the poverty and desolation are gradually replaced by delightful reading, school, studying, and finally publishing, Hurston's narrative becomes brighter. Her success, of course, comes mostly through her own ambition and determination, but part of it, at least, is made possible by the number of influential people, whom she recognizes in a chapter called "Friendship," who helped her. Among these are Charles S. Johnson, who published her first short stories in *Opportunity*; Franz Boas, who encouraged her to continue her studies in Anthropology, and arranged for her to collect folklore in the South; Fannie Hurst, who hired her as secretary, chauffeur, and entertainer; Annie Nathan Meyer, who helped to get her a scholarship to Barnard College from whence she graduated in

1928; Mrs. R. Osgood Mason, who financed many of her ventures; and Ethel Waters, whose friendship Hurston valued all her life.

With so many good things following so many bad things, Hurston achieved a growing aura:

> I felt the warm embrace of kin and kind for the first time since the night of my mother's funeral, when we had huddled about the organ all sodden and bewildered, with the walls of our home suddenly blown down. . . . But now, that was all over. (181)

The second half of *Dust Tracks on a Road* is permeated with this aura as Hurston writes of research, love, religion, her books, and her race. Each section is engaging, enlightening, often troubling as it reveals something new about its author. Hurston herself emerges as an overwhelming personality who speaks her mind about everything. Her sister Sarah, she writes, "was struggling along with a husband for whom we all wished a short sickness and a quick funeral." Of her father, she writes: "Old Maker had left out the steering gear when He gave Papa his talents." Thus, Hurston and her autobiography well earned their description by the *New York Times* as "saucy, defiant, high-pressure . . . as vivid as jasmine and as vulgar as a well-liquored fish-fry." Hurston had come a long way. No matter what her success, however, she never forgot her humble beginnings:

> Booker T. Washington said once that you must not judge a man by the heights to which he has risen, but by the depths from which he came. So to me these honors meant something, insignificant as they might appear to the world. It was a long step for the waif of Eatonville. From the depth of my inner heart I appreciated the fact that the world had not been altogether unkind to Mama's child. (180)

VI   *"The Best Fiction She Ever Wrote"*

Those who knew Zora or who have come to know her through her works believe that her autobiography rings a bit false. In his introduction to the 1969 edition of *Dust Tracks on a Road*, Darwin Turner, who has been occasionally hostile toward Hurston, calls the book "perhaps the best fiction she ever wrote,"[19] later arguing in his own book, *In a Minor Chord*, that *Dust Tracks on a Road* illustrates Hurston's "artful candor and coy reticence, her contradictions and silences, her irrationalities and extravagant boasts which plead for the world to recognize and respect her."[20] Alice Walker said Zora "is probably more honest in her fieldwork and her fiction, than she is in her autobiography, because she was hesitant to reveal how different she really was,"[21] while Arna Bontemps noted that "Miss Hurston deals very simply with the more serious aspects of Negro life in America—she ignores them."[22] Harold Preece called the book "the tragedy of a gifted, sensitive mind, eaten up by an egocentrism fed on the patronizing admiration of the dominant white world,"[23] and Robert Hemenway admits that the book can be "discomfiting" because "like much of her career, it often appears contradictory. Zora seems to be both an advocate for the universal, demonstrating that this black woman does not look at the world in racial terms, and the celebrant of a unique ethnic upbringing in an all-black village."[24] Hemenway continues: "When Zora selects a story from the repertoire of her life and narrates it for her audience, *Dust Tracks on a Road* succeeds. It fails when she tries to shape the narrative into a statement of universality, manipulating events and ideas in order to suggest that the personal voyage of Zora Neale Hurston is something more than the special experience of one black woman."[25]

In order to judge Hurston fairly (indeed, if we must judge her at all), it is necessary to consider the material her publishers insisted that she leave out of the book. The manuscript can be found at the Beinecke, Yale University Library. Some of the material is clearly libelous and should have been excised, but her rather biting statements on race relations, democracy, and America in general should have been included in the published version. That way those readers who feel that Zora was not socially and racially conscious would have been soundly rebuffed. Zora was a black author in a white publishing world, it is to be remembered, and, like Paul Laurence Dunbar and Charles Chesnutt, she was subject to the constraints of her editors, who were subject to the constraints of a predominantly white reading audience who did not cherish being offended or reminded of the "sins" of their fathers. As Zora once told an interviewer from the *New York Amsterdam News*, "rather than get across all of the things which you want to say you must compromise and work within the limitations [of those people] who have the final authority in deciding whether or not a book shall be printed."[26] In confirmation of Zora's assessment, a Lippincott editor wrote across the bottom of one of Zora's manuscript pages: "Suggest eliminating international opinions as irrelevant to autobiography."[27]

In the manuscript version of *Dust Tracks on a Road*, Zora speaks openly and knowledgeably about colonialism and the oppression that usually accompanies it: "All around me, bitter tears are being shed over the fate of Holland, Belgium, France and England. I must confess to being a little dry around the eyes. I hear people shaking with shudders at the thought of Germany collecting taxes in Holland. I have not heard a word against Holland collecting one-twelfth of poor people's wages in Asia." In another passage, she takes a cut at the practices of Roosevelt: "President Roosevelt could extend his four freedoms to some people right here in America. . . . I am not bitter, but I see what I see. He can call names across an ocean, but he evidently has not the courage to speak even softly at home. . . . I will fight for my country but I will not lie for her." About democracy, she says: "As I see it, the doctrines of democracy deal with the aspirations of men's souls, but the application deals with things. One hand in somebody else's pocket and one on your gun and you are highly civilized. Your heart is where it belongs—in your pocket book. Put it in your bosom and you are backward. Desire enough for your own use and you are a heathen." About whites' attitudes of superiority, Zora says it "would be a good thing for the Anglo-Saxon to get the idea out of his head that everybody owes him something just for being blonde. I am forced to the conclusion that two-thirds of them do hold that view. The idea of human slavery is so deeply ground in that the pink-toes can't get it out of their system."[28]

In the published version of a chapter entitled "My People, My People," Zora speaks of the paradoxes inherent in being black. As a child she was confused over phrases like "race consciousness," "race pride," and "race solidarity" that gushed forth from black orators' mouths. According to these orators, "(a) The Negro had made the greatest progress in fifty years of any race on the face of the globe. (b) Negroes composed the most *beautiful* race on earth, being just like a flower garden with every color and kind. (c) Negroes were the bravest men on earth, facing every danger like lions, and fighting with demons." She wondered how to reconcile these phrases with the black folktales she had heard about black people being monkeys or with the jokes she often heard about dark-skinned blacks, particularly black women. These apparent contradictions led to probing questions: "Were Negroes the great heroes I heard about from the platform, or were they the ridiculous monkeys of everyday talk? Was it really honorable to be black?"

Significantly, Zora was also puzzled over black reaction to the 1954 Supreme Court decision: "The whole matter revolves around the self-respect of my people. How much satisfaction can I get from a court order for somebody to associate with me who does not wish me near them. . . . It is a contradiction in terms to scream race pride and equality while at the same time spurning Negro teachers and self-association."[29] A local incident provided some answers for Zora. One night her father and his friends, though tense and afraid, had armed themselves and gone to rescue another friend reportedly held by the Ku Klux Klan. When they discovered that the piercing cries they had heard were coming from a white and not one of their black brothers, they mocked the victim and laughed. Zora interpreted the incident this way: "They had gone out to rescue a neighbor or die in the attempt, and they were back with their families. So they let loose their insides and laughed. . . . The men who spoke of members of their race as monkeys had gone out to die for one. The men who were always saying, 'My skin-folks, but not kinfolks; my race but not my taste,' had rushed forth to die for one of these same contemptibles. . . . So I could see that what looked like ridicule was really the Negro poking a little fun at himself. At the same time, just like other people, hoping and wishing he was what the orators said he was" (239).

Zora has been lampooned the most because she seemed to ignore race prejudice in America. She had said in the last paragraph of *Dust Tracks on a Road* that "I have no race prejudice of any kind. My kinfolks, and my 'skin-folks' are dearly loved." She claimed that she saw "the same virtues and vices everywhere I look." She had refused to write about the Race Problem, excusing herself with, "My interest lies in what makes a man or a woman do such and so, regardless of his color," though racial issues invariably surface in her novels. However much she may have wanted to transcend racial prejudices—in the unpublished manuscript of *Dust Tracks on a Road* she admits that race prejudice exists not only in America but all over the world, but that she turns her back on the past, wants to get on with the present—she was very much aware of them. In the same month that her autobiography was published, for instance, incensed by the treatment of blacks at a Signal Corps school set up for them at Florida Normal, she wrote to Walter White, then president of the NAACP: "Well, the Negroes have been bitched again! . . . It is awful, Walter. The Government having been forced by you to grant this Signal Corp to Negroes, dumped it in this little hole, and felt that your mouth was stopped. Remember that this is the ONLY one for Negroes in the U.S., though the whites have several. I feel that the whole body of Negroes are being insulted and mocked. . . . I am only giving you a *hint*. There is plenty here to find out. It concerns us all, and I really think something ought to be done."[30]

Fanny Hurst has said that Zora "seemed to have very little indignation for the imposed status of her race," probably because "her awakening powers and subsequent recognition tended to act as a soporific to her early sufferings and neglect."[31] Hurst records an incident where she and Zora visited Eatonville and Zora rather self-righteously remarked, "Everybody in this town had the same chance to work themselves out of it that I did." When Hurst countered, "But not your talents," Zora replied, "Then let them use elbow grease for what they are fitted to do. I used it when I had to. I scrubbed and dish-washed. The world will treat you right if you are all right." In her relations with Zora, however, Hurst found that "in spite of herself her rich heritage cropped out not only in her personality but more importantly in her writings." Too, as Hurst documents, Zora experienced race prejudice often enough. When Zora and Fanny traveled together, "At hotels, Zora was either assigned to servants' quarters or informed that they were full up." On the other hand, when Hurst claimed that Zora was a princess, they both received the best of treatment. After one meal achieved through these deceptive, though successful, tactics, Zora remarked, "Who would think that a good meal could be so bitter."[32] Obviously Zora knew all the time that the world would often treat you wrong no matter how "all right" you were.

Finally, of course, there's that suggestive, ambivalent, ironic last paragraph of *Dust Tracks on a Road* that must be reckoned with:

I have no race prejudice of any kind. My kinfolks, and my "skin-folks" are dearly loved. My own circumference of everyday life is there. But I see their same virtues and vices everywhere I look. So I give you all my right hand of fellowship and love, and hope for the same from you. In my eyesight, you lose nothing by not looking just like me. I will remember you all in my good thoughts, and I ask you kindly to do the same for me. Not only just me. You, who play the zig-zag lightning of power over the world, with the grumbling thunder in your wake, think kindly of those who walk in the dust. And you who walk in humble places, think kindly too, of others. There has been no proof in the world so far that you would be less arrogant if you held the lever of power in your hands. Let us all be kissing-friends. Consider that with tolerance and patience, we godly demons may breed a noble world in a few hundred generations or so. Maybe all of us who do not have the good fortune to meet, or meet again, in this world, will meet at a barbecue. (293–94)

Ann Rayson says that "said any other way, a comment like this would elicit considerable hostility from friends and foes alike. But through style alone she can get away with saying things for which a straight [black] conservative [George Schuyler, for instance] could never be forgiven."[33] Hemenway is quick to point out, however, that

like a member of the American Indian Movement telling whites at a bicentennial celebration that he is pleased the American immigrants could visit his country as guests for these past 200 years, Zora assures whites that they do not have to feel inferior just because they do not look like her. By ironically reversing the perspective, exposing the presumed standard of beauty, she documents the absurdity of the white norm. . . . Yet there is also a final twist, a concealed irony, that leaves one wondering just where both author and reader now find themselves. "A few hundred generations or so" is sufficiently futuristic to imply that the vision will never come true; the proximity of "godly demons" and "barbecue" causes one to think of Hades. Is Zora really telling her readers, [most of whom, of course, were white], "I'll see you in Hell"? Is it the fire next time?[34]

Indeed it may be. Zora Hurston, with arms akimbo, hat rakishly cocked, and legs spread wide, may have been preparing for battle even as she wrote those final words. The opening invective of the letter to White—"Well, the Negroes have been bitched again!"—suggests that she had already sharpened her tools.

Hurston's nonfiction is, for the most part, just as engaging as her fiction. It is certainly just as important. The same engaging personality, the same revealing language, are overwhelmingly present in both, and both are important for the contributions they make to the world of literature. In her nonfiction one perceives the matrix of her fiction, "the seeds that sprouted and the cankers that destroyed."[35] Any study of Zora Neale Hurston and her works, then, is incomplete without a thorough consideration of *Mules and Men*, *Tell My Horse*, and *Dust Tracks on a Road*.

CHAPTER 9

Conclusion

THERE is no indication that Zora N. Hurston was ever well known—as a writer or as a person—among the masses during her lifetime. With an impressive group of people—the elitists—on the other hand, she enjoyed brief periods of notoriety: "She had been granted honorary doctorates, published in national magazines, featured on the cover of the *Saturday Review*, invited to speak at major universities, and praised by the *New York Herald Tribune* as being 'in the front rank' not only of black writers but of all American writers. She had been the most important collector of Afro-American folklore in the country. She had published more books than any other black American woman."[1] In spite of this, however, she seemed to feel it necessary to best herself. She was seldom satisfied with her output, never satisfied with the quality of what she had written. After the publication of each of her major works, including *Seraph on the Suwanee*, her last published novel, she confided in one or another of her friends that "I am not so sure that I have done my best, but I tried. I need not tell you that my goal still eludes me. I am in despair because it keeps ever ahead of me." To herself, she was a failure. Fortunately, no critic wholly supports this view. While a few lampoon her for what they consider her lack of social consciousness, her tendency to transcend racism and prejudices by disallowing them a major role in her works, and for technical and narrative deficiences in her fiction, most praise her for her ability to tell a good story well, for her vivid and unforgettable figurative language, for her staunch individualism, and for the sense of "racial health" that permeates her fiction.

170

I *Critical Assessments*

Robert Bone was among the first to recognize Hurston's value. In *The Negro Novel in America*, he praises Hurston, along with George Wylie Henderson, for realizing and exploring "the literary possibilities of the canefield and the cotton patch." While he condemns *Jonah's Gourd Vine* for having "style without structure, a rich verbal texture without dramatic form, 'atmosphere' without real characterization," he calls *Their Eyes Were Watching God* "possibly the best novel of the period, excepting *Native Son*."[2] In *Down Home*, Bone calls *Moses, Man of the Mountain* a "brilliant allegory" in the picaresque tradition.[3]

Sterling Brown, Benjamin Brawley, Hugh Gloster, and Nick Aaron Ford allow Hurston a few pages in their books but, more often than not, they find her lacking in some of the necessary qualities for a successful black novelist. Their comments generally turn upon Hurston's "whitewashed" treatment of black life and, in Ford's case, her failure to fully develop her characters, particularly John Pearson of *Jonah's Gourd Vine*.

Darwin T. Turner, who devotes the last third of *In a Minor Chord* to Hurston whom he calls a "wandering minstrel," presents a largely negative view of Hurston the person, but he tempers this with a primarily favorable view of Hurston the writer. He calls Hurston the individual "an imaginative, somewhat shallow, woman, desperate for recognition and reassurance to assuage her feelings of inferiority; a blind follower of that social code which approves arrogance toward one's assumed peers and inferiors but requires total psychological commitment to a subservient posture before one's supposed superiors." Of the writer he says: "Her novels deserve more recognition than they have received. . . . Gifted with an ear for dialect, an appreciation of the folktale, a lively imagination, and an understanding of feminine psychology, she interwove these materials in deceptively simple stories which exhibit increasing artistic consciousness and her awareness of the shifting tastes in the American literary market." Turner concludes his study of Hurston with comments that do Hurston more harm than good:

Because of her simple style, humor, and folklore, Zora Neale Hurston deserves more recognition than she ever earned. But, superficial and shallow in her artistic and social judgments, she became neither an impeccable raconteur nor a scholar. Always, she remained a wandering minstrel. It was eccentric but perhaps appropriate for her to return to Florida to take a job as a cook and maid for a white family and to die in poverty. She had not ended her days as she once had hoped—a farmer among the growing things she loved. Instead she had returned to the level of life which she proposed for her people.[4]

Fortunately, Robert Hemenway, Hurston's biographer, had access to information that Turner must not have seen. He gives a more sympathetic reading of Hurston:

Personally, Zora Hurston was a complex woman with a high tolerance for contradiction. She could occasionally manipulate people to aid her career, and she was a natural actress who could play many roles. Physically, she was a high-energy person, capable of intense work for long stretches of time, possessed of a personal effervescence that frequently overwhelmed. She had an instinct for publicity, and she was capable of commercially popularizing black culture, of taking white friends to storefront churches, telling down-home stories to those wishing to romanticize black life. Above all, she was a sophisticated writer who was never afraid to be herself. She was flamboyant and yet vulnerable, self-centered and yet kind, a Republican conservative and yet an early black nationalist. Her personality could seem a series of opposites, and her friends were often incapable of reconciling the polarities of her personal style. . . . There was always, however, a central pattern to the crazy quilt. Hurston remained committed to her work, and to the honest portraiture of her race, no matter how poorly that commitment paid.
Zora Neale Hurston was a nontragic person, a woman who rejoiced in print about the beauty of being black. When her blues came, when bigots and rednecks and crackers and liberals and racial missionaries got her down, she retreated into a privacy that protected her sense of self; publicly, she avoided confrontation by announcing that she didn't look at a person's color, only one's worth. She personally believed in an integrated society, but she spent her career trying to preserve and celebrate black cultural practices. Her life testifies only for her particular black experience, but her career witnesses for contemporary black authors. Why did such a writer end up living on food vouchers from the state of Florida? Why did

her body lie in wait for subscriptions to pay for a funeral? The answers are as complicated as her art, as paradoxical as her person, as simple as the fact that she lived in a country that fails to honor its black artists.[5]

II A Resurrection

To date, a number of articles—somewhere in the neighborhood of twenty—have been written about Hurston and her accomplishments (see bibliography). That is not an impressive number when one considers that there have been occasions for such articles since the 1920s when Zora began her career. The majority of the articles have appeared since 1970 and mark a decided resurgence of interest in the "Ethnographer" of Eatonville.

In 1973, Alice Walker went to Florida to search out Hurston's unmarked grave and place a marker there. It hardly matters that Walker could never be certain that she had found the right grave (weeds in the graveyard were waist-high, graves sunken, most unmarked); what is more important is that whoever reads the tombstone—

ZORA NEALE HURSTON
"A Genius of the South"
1901 – – – 1960
Novelist, Folklorist
Anthropologist

—cannot fail to know Hurston's importance.

In 1975, the Modern Language Association thought Hurston important enough to offer a Zora Neale Hurston seminar, and by that time, Hemenway was nearing the end of his cross-country research trek in search of Hurston. His loving biography was published in November 1977. In 1979, Alice Walker and the Feminist Press published *I Love Myself When I Am Laughing* ...., an anthology of Hurston's most impressive works. Now the University of Florida offers a Zora N. Hurston fellowship in anthropology, and the city of Orlando, Florida, boasts a Zora Neale Hurston building.

In the final analysis, however, Hurston will live on in her

works—her four novels, two books of folklore, autobiography, numerous short stories, essays, and articles—and in the works of those who remember her well—Langston Hughes, Fannie Hurst, Carl Van Vechten. That she has risen from relative obscurity is an assurance that an important part of Afro-American tradition will not die and that we as a people take our duty seriously: "*We are a people. A people do not throw their geniuses away. If they do, it is our duty as witnesses for the future* to collect them again for the sake of our children. If necessary, bone by bone."[6]

Alice Walker, a natural and literary descendant of Hurston and a tradition bearer in her own right, praises Zora's work for its "racial health—a sense of black people as complete, complex, *undiminished* human beings, a sense that is lacking in so much black writing and literature." According to Walker,

Zora was before her time—in intellectual circles—in the lifestyle she chose. By the sixties everyone understood that black women could wear beautiful cloths on their beautiful heads and care about the authenticity of things cullud *and* African. By the sixties it was no longer a crime to receive financial assistance, in the form of grants and fellowships, for one's work. (Interestingly, those writers who complained that Zora "got money from white folks" were often themselves totally supported, down to the food they ate—or, in Langston Hughes's case, *tried* to eat, after his white "godmother" discarded him—by white patrons.) By the sixties, nobody cared that marriage didn't last forever. No one expected it to. And I do believe that now, in the seventies, we do not expect (though we may wish and pray) every black person who speaks to *always* speak *correctly* (since this is impossible); or if we *do* expect it, we deserve all the silent leadership we are likely to get.[7]

Hurston was undeniably before her time. She loved hard and unhesitatingly, though the brevity of her marriages belies this fact; she was a black nationalist when black nationalists were being discredited and deported. What really made her premature, however, was all the beauty and struggle of *Their Eyes Were Watching God* where marriage is largely defined in sexual terms; where one mate must remain petal open and honest for the other; where mere sex may take place without consummation of the marriage since consummation only takes place when the right dust-bearing bee comes along; where the quality of one's life counts more than the quantity of it; where poetry is more essential than prose, love more essential than money, sharing paramount to dominating; where one's dream is the horizon and one must "go there to know there." All that and more made Hurston extraordinary; all that makes the beauty of *Their Eyes Were Watching God* almost unbearable today, makes one wonder if even today the world is ready for Zora Neale Hurston.

Her works are important because they affirm blackness (while not denying whiteness) in a black-denying society. They present characters who are not all lovable but who are undeniably and realistically human. They record the history, the life, of a place and time which are remarkably like other places and times, though perhaps a bit more honest in the rendering. They offer some light for those who "ain't ne'er seen de light at all."

In spite of, if not because of, the mystery which surrounds her, Zora Neale Hurston has become a star of late, steadily twinkling hither and yonder casting her folkloric beams to show her awed followers the way. Fannie Hurst said of Zora, "We rejoice that she passed this way so brightly but alas, too briefly." Clearly, the unpredictable, unfathomable Zora has run the muck-de-muck over Hurst. She walks brightly among us now. Her truth marches on.

Notes and References

Chapter One

1. The 1969 Arno Press and *New York Times* Reprint of the 1942 edition of *Dust Tracks on a Road* has been used throughout. Everette Hurston shared his opinions in an interview with me during the summer of 1978. In spite of the brother's comments and extensive research, the uncertainty about Zora's correct birthdate remains. Perhaps it really isn't all that significant, however; as Zora says in *Dust Tracks on a Road*, "maybe some of the details of my birth as told me might be a little inaccurate, but it is pretty well established that I really did get born."

2. *Dust Tracks on a Road*, p. 37.

3. Information obtained during interview with Everette Hurston.

4. *Dust Tracks on a Road*, p. 20.

5. Ibid., p. 11.

6. Zora claims to have been nine when her mother died. This would make the year of Zora's birth 1895.

7. Robert Bone, "The Harlem Renaissance: A Reappraisal," *Down Home* (New York, 1975), p. 119.

8. *Dust Tracks on a Road*, pp. 102–103.

9. Ibid., p. 132.

10. Ibid., p. 124.

11. Ibid., pp. 158–59.

12. Robert Hemenway, *Zora Neale Hurston: A Literary Biography* (Chicago, 1977), p. 94.

13. Zora gives Charles S. Johnson credit for starting the Harlem Renaissance (see *Dust Tracks on a Road*, p. 176). According to Zora, Johnson was too reticent to take credit for all that he had done.

14. Langston Hughes, *The Big Sea* (New York, 1940), pp. 244–45.

15. Fannie Hurst, "Zora Neale Hurston: A Personality Sketch," *Yale University Library Gazette* 35 (1960): 17.

16. Hughes, *The Big Sea*, p. 239.

17. *Dust Tracks on a Road*, pp. 69–70.

18. Hemenway, pp. 21–22.

19. Franz Boas to Carter G. Woodson, November 6, 18, December

7, 1926; Woodson to Boas, February 17, 1927, as quoted in Hemenway, p. 84.

20. *Dust Tracks on a Road*, pp. 182–83.

21. Ibid.

22. Hughes, *The Big Sea*, p. 325.

23. The contract is part of the Hurston papers in the Alain Locke Collection, Howard University Library.

24. Ibid.

25. *Dust Tracks on a Road*, p. 206.

26. Hurston to Mason, October 10, 1931, and February 29, 1932, respectively. Locke Collection, Howard University.

27. Alain Locke Collection, Howard University.

28. Ibid.

29. I am indebted to Hemenway, p. 177, for this quotation.

30. Hurston to Mason, January 14, 1932. Locke Collection.

31. Hurston to Mason, October 15, 1931. Locke Collection.

32. Hurston to Mason, January 6, 1932. Locke Collection.

33. Hurston to Mason, April 4, 1932. Locke Collection.

34. Hurston to Mason, May 17, 1932. Locke Collection.

35. Hurston to Mason, May 17, 1932. Locke Collection.

36. Hurston to Mason, July 6, 1932. Locke Collection.

37. Hughes to Arthur Spingarn, January 21, 1931. Arthur Spingarn Collection, Howard University.

38. Ibid.

39. Hemenway says that the two met in September. Hughes, in letter to Spingarn, January 21, 1931, says it was November.

40. Hughes to Spingarn, January 21, 1931. Spingarn Collection.

41. Hughes to Spingarn, January 30, 1931. Spingarn Collection.

42. Hurston to Mason, February 3, 1931. Locke Collection.

43. After Hurston's death, Hughes did permit the third act to be published in *Drama Critique*.

44. Hemenway, p. 156.

Chapter Two

1. Bertram Lippincott to Carl Van Vechten, February 1, 1934. James Weldon Johnson Collection, Yale University Library.

2. Hurston to Carl Van Vechten, March 24, 1934. James W. Johnson Collection, Yale University Library.

3. *Dust Tracks on a Road*, p. 214.

4. Stanley J. Kunitz and Howard Haycraft, *Twentieth Century Authors* (New York, 1942), p. 695.

5. John O'Brien, ed., *Interviews with Black Writers* (New York, 1973), p. 202.

6. Hurston to James W. Johnson, May 8, 1934. James W. Johnson Collection, Yale University Library.

7. Hurston to Thomas E. Jones, October 12, 1934, Fisk University, as quoted in Hemenway, pp. 201–202; Hurston to Alain Locke, March 24, 1934. Locke Collection, Howard University.

8. Hurston to Carl Van Vechten, March 24, 1934, Johnson Collection, Yale University Library.

9. Hurston to Van Vechten, September 6, 1935, Johnson Collection, Yale University Library.

10. Hurston to Moe, July 6, 1937, as quoted in Hemenway, p. 247.

11. Hurston to Moe, August 6, 1937; quoted in Hemenway, p. 248.

12. Harold Courlander, *Saturday Review*, October 15, 1938, p. 6.

13. Hemenway, p. 252.

14. Ibid.

15. Hemenway, p. 256.

16. Ibid., pp. 215, 270.

17. Darwin T. Turner, *In a Minor Chord* (Carbondale, Illinois, 1971), p. 109.

18. Alain Locke, "Dry Fields and Green Pastures," *Opportunity* 18 (January 1940): 7.

19. Ralph Ellison, "Recent Negro Fiction," *New Masses*, August 5, 1941, p. 211.

20. Hurston to Van Vechten, James W. Johnson Collection, Yale University Library.

21. Lippincott to Van Vechten, October 4, 1939, Johnson Collection, Yale University Library.

22. Hemenway, p. 274.

23. Hurston to Holt, February 11, 1943. University of Florida Papers, Gainesville.

24. Unpublished *Dust Tracks* manuscript, Johnson Collection, Yale University Library.

25. Ibid.

26. Arna Bontemps, "From Eatonville, Fla. to Harlem," *New York Herald Tribune*, November 23, 1942.

27. Harold Preece, "The Negro Folk Cult," *Crisis* 43 (1936): 364, 374.

28. "The Watchtower," *New York Amsterdam News*, February 27, 1943.

29. *Negro Digest* (*Black World*) 4 (December 1945): 45–48.

30. Lester B. Granger, *California Eagle*, December 20, 1951.

31. Hurston to White, November 24, 1942, Johnson Collection, Yale University Library.

32. Hurston to Rawlings, May 16, 1943, University of Florida Papers.

33. *New York Amsterdam News*, November 18, 1944.

34. Hurston to Van Vechten, Johnson Collection, Yale University Library.

35. Ibid.

36. *Pittsburgh Courier*, September 28, 1946.

37. Hurston to Van Vechten, July 30, 1947, Johnson Collection, Yale University Library.

38. Hurston to Rawlings, n.d., University of Florida Papers.

39. Hurston to Van Vechten, October 30, 1948, Johnson Collection, Yale University Library.

40. Hemenway, p. 326.

41. Hurston to Margrit Sabloniere, March 15, 1956, University of Florida Papers.

42. June Jordan, "Notes toward a Balancing of Love and Hatred," *Black World* 23:10 (August 1974): 242.

43. Hurston to Waterbury; quoted in Hemenway, p. 338.

44. Hurston to Van Vechten, Johnson Collection, Yale University Library.

45. Phone conversation with Cutler, July 30, 1977, Gainesville, Florida.

46. Hurston to Sabloniere, December 3, 1955, University of Florida Papers.

47. Hurston to Harper Bros., January 16, 1959, University of Florida Papers.

48. "Introduction," *Dust Tracks on a Road* (New York, 1969), pp. ii–iii.

49. Van Vechten to Fannie Hurst, July 5, 1960, Johnson Collection, Yale University Library.

50. Hemenway, p. 5.

Chapter Three

1. Robert Bone, "Three Versions of Pastoral," *Down Home*, pp. 139–40.

2. *Dust Tracks on a Road*, pp. 71–72.

3. Bone, p. 144.

4. Ralph Ellison, "The Art of Fiction: An Interview," *Shadow and Act* (New York, 1972), p. 171.

5. *Dust Tracks on a Road*, p. 176.

6. Bone, p. 145.

7. Hurston, "How It Feels to Be Colored Me," *World Tomorrow* 11 (May 1928): 215–16.

8. *Dust Tracks on a Road*, p. 53.

9. Hemenway, p. 11.

10. Hurston, *Color Struck, Fire!!* 1 (November 1926): 7–15.

11. Hemenway, p. 68.

12. Hurston, "How It Feels to Be Colored Me," pp. 215–16.

13. Bone, p. 149.

14. See Lillie P. Howard, "Marriage: Zora Neale Hurston's System of Values," *CLA Journal* 21:2 (December 1977): 256–68.

15. Bone, p. 144.

16. Ellison, p. 171.

Chapter Four

1. All references are to *Jonah's Gourd Vine*, rpt., New York, 1971. Page numbers are cited in the text.

2. *Dust Tracks on a Road*, p. 214.

3. Ibid.

4. Ibid.

5. James W. Johnson Collection, Yale University Library.

6. Larry Neal, "Introduction," *Jonah's Gourd Vine* (New York, 1971), pp. 6–7.

7. Hemenway, p. 200.

8. Ibid.

9. Nick Aaron Ford, *Contemporary Negro Novel* (rpt., College Park, Md., 1968), p. 99.

10. Neal, p. 7.

11. Johnson Collection, Yale University Library.

12. John Chamberlain, review of *Jonah's Gourd Vine, New York Times*, May 3, 1934, p. 7.

13. Hurston to Johnson, May 8, 1934, Johnson Collection. The review was by John Chamberlain, *New York Times*, May 3, 1934, p. 7.

14. Hemenway, p. 200.

15. *In a Minor Chord*, p. 105.

16. Hemenway, p. 201.

Chapter Five

1. All page references in the text are to the University of Illinois 1978 reprint of *Their Eyes Were Watching God*.

2. Robert Bone, *The Negro Novel in America* (New Haven, 1965), pp. 126–32.

3. Hemenway, p. 232.

4. *Dust Tracks on a Road*, p. 268.

5. Hemenway, p. 231.

6. *In a Minor Chord*, p. 106.

7. Bone, p. 130.

8. James R. Giles, "The Significance of Time in Zora Neale Hurston's *Their Eyes Were Watching God*," *Negro American Literary Forum* 6:2 (Summer 1972): 52–53, 60.

9. Hemenway, p. 9.

10. Ellease Southerland, "The Novelist-Anthropologist's Life/Works," *Black World* 23:10 (August 1974): 26.

11. The dozens is a folkloristic game, popular among blacks, which consists of a verbal exchange of insults between two players.

12. Giles, p. 52.

13. Ibid.

14. Southerland, p. 27.

15. June Jordan, "Notes toward a Balancing of Love and Hatred," *Black World* 24:10 (August 1974): 6.

16. Ibid.

17. Giles, p. 53.

18. Ibid.

Chapter Six

1. All page references in the text are to the 1967 Chatham Bookseller reprint of the 1939 Lippincott edition of *Moses, Man of the Mountain*.

2. *In a Minor Chord*, p. 109.

3. Ibid., p. 111.

4. Blyden Jackson, "Some Negroes in the Land of Goshen," *Tennessee Folklore Society Bulletin* 19 (December 1953): 103–107.

5. Ann Rayson, "The Novels of Zora Neale Hurston," *Studies in Black Literature* 5:3 (Winter 1974): 1–10.

6. Ibid.

7. Ibid.

8. Hemenway, p. 215.

9. Ibid., p. 260.

10. Ibid., pp. 270–71.

11. Ibid., p. 260.

12. Both *Ol' Man Adam and His Chillun* (1928) and *The Green*

Pastures (1930) are possible sources for *Moses, Man of the Mountain*. Whether Hurston was familiar with either is unknown, though there are similarities between her work and those of Bradford and Connelly.

13. Rayson, p. 5.
14. *Dust Tracks on a Road*, pp. 285–87.
15. Evelyn T. Helmick, "Zora Neale Hurston," *Carrell* 11:1, 2 (June-December 1970): 1–19.
16. Rayson, p. 5.
17. Hemenway, p. 270.
18. Turner, p. 111.
19. Jackson, p. 106.
20. Rayson, pp. 6–7.
21. Ibid.
22. Bertram Lippincott to Carl Van Vechten, October 4, 1939, Johnson Collection, Yale University Library.
23. Alain Locke, "Dry Fields and Green Pastures," *Opportunity* 18 (January 1940): 7.
24. Ralph Ellison, "Recent Negro Fiction," *New Masses,* August 5, 1941, p. 211.
25. Hurston to Edwin Grover, October 12, 1939, University of Florida Papers.

Chapter Seven

1. All page references in the text are to *Seraph on the Suwanee* (New York, 1948).
2. Quoted in Hemenway, p. 308.
3. Hurston to Van Vechten, November 2, 1942, Johnson Collection, Yale University Library.
4. Hemenway, p. 307.
5. Bone, *The Negro Novel in America*, p. 169.
6. Turner, *In a Minor Chord*, p. 111.
7. Hurston to Burroughs Mitchell, October 1947; quoted in Hemenway, p. 310.
8. Hurston to Mitchell, as quoted in Hemenway, p. 312. Hemenway obtained his information from the Hurston files at Scribner's.
9. Hemenway, p. 314.
10. Turner, p. 111.
11. Hemenway, p. 315.
12. *Dust Tracks on a Road*, pp. 220–21.

Chapter Eight

1. All page references are to the Negro Universities Press 1969 reprint of *Mules and Men*.

2. All references to *Tell My Horse* are based on the Lippincott edition, 1938.

3. All references to *Dust Tracks on a Road* are based upon the 1969 Arno Press and *New York Times* reprint.

4. Hurston to Van Vechten, March 24, 1934, Johnson Collection.

5. Sterling Brown, *The Negro in American Fiction* (Washington, D.C., 1937) pp. 159–61.

6. Brown, review of *Mules and Men*, unidentified newspaper clipping, February 25, 1936, Johnson Collection, Yale University Library.

7. Ibid.

8. Richard Wright, "In Between Laughter and Tears," *New Masses*, October 5, 1937, pp. 22, 25.

9. Preece, "The Negro Folk Cult," *Crisis* 43 (1936): 364, 374.

10. *Twentieth Century Authors*, p. 695.

11. Hurston to Henry Allen Moe, n.d. [received April 20, 1936], quoted in Hemenway, p. 228, (Guggenheim Foundation).

12. Benjamin Brawley, *The Negro Genius* (New York, 1937), pp. 258–59.

13. Harold Courlander, *Saturday Review*, October 15, 1938, p. 6.

14. James W. Byrd, "Zora Neale Hurston: A Novel Folklorist," *Tennessee Folklore Society Bulletin* 21 (1955): 37–41.

15. Turner, "Introduction," *Dust Tracks on a Road* (New York, 1969), p. iv.

16. Hemenway, p. 277.

17. Hurston to Hamilton Holt, February 1, 1943, University of Florida Papers.

18. Actually, Zora might have been much older. See Chapter 1.

19. Turner, p. iv. Actually, Turner is quoting "someone" here. The exact quote from his introduction is: "But, as someone once said, *Dust Tracks on a Road* may be the best fiction Zora Neale Hurston ever wrote."

20. Turner, *In a Minor Chord*, p. 91.

21. *Interviews with Black Writers*, p. 204.

22. Arna Bontemps, review of *Dust Tracks on a Road, Books*, November 22, 1942.

23. Preece, *"Dust Tracks on a Road,"* *Tomorrow*, February 1943.

24. Hemenway, p. 276.

25. Ibid., p. 277.

26. "Zora Neale Hurston Reveals Key to Her Literary Success," *New York Amsterdam News*, November 18, 1944.

27. Unpublished *Dust Tracks on a Road* Manuscript, Johnson Collection, Yale University Library.

28. Ibid.

29. *Orlando Sentinel*, August 22, 1955.

30. Hurston to Walter White, November 24, 1942, Johnson Collection, Yale University Library.

31. Hurst, *Yale University Library Gazette* 35 (1960): 17–22.

32. Ibid.

33. Ann Rayson, "*Dust Tracks on a Road*: Zora Neale Hurston and the Form of Black Autobiography," *Negro American Literature Forum* 7 (Summer 1973): 39.

34. Hemenway, p. 286.

35. Turner, *In a Minor Chord*, p. 91.

Chapter Nine

1. Hemenway, p. 4.

2. Bone, *The Negro Novel in America*, pp. 123, 127–28.

3. Bone, *Down Home*, p. 114.

4. Turner, *In a Minor Chord*, pp. 98, 120.

5. Hemenway, pp. 5–7.

6. Alice Walker, "Foreword" to Robert Hemenway, *Zora Neale Hurston: A Literary Biography* (Chicago, 1977), p. xviii.

7. Ibid., pp. xv–xvi.

Selected Bibliography

PRIMARY SOURCES

1. Books

Jonah's Gourd Vine. Philadelphia: J. B. Lippincott, 1934. Reprinted, with an introduction by Larry Neal, Philadelphia: J. B. Lippincott, 1971.

Mules and Men. Philadelphia: J. B. Lippincott, 1935. Reprinted, New York: Negro Universities Press, 1969. Reprinted, with an introduction by Darwin Turner, New York: Harper and Row, 1970.

Their Eyes Were Watching God. Philadelphia: J. B. Lippincott, 1937. Reprinted, Greenwich, Conn.: Fawcett Publications, 1965. Reprinted, New York: Negro Universities Press, 1969. Reprinted, Urbana: University of Illinois Press, 1978.

Tell My Horse. Philadelphia: J. B. Lippincott, 1938.

Moses, Man of the Mountain. Philadelphia: J. B. Lippincott, 1939. Reprinted, Chatham, N.J.: Chatham Bookseller, 1974.

Dust Tracks on a Road. Philadelphia: J. B. Lippincott, 1942. Reprinted, with an introduction by Darwin Turner, New York: Arno Press, 1969. Reprinted, with an introduction by Larry Neal, New York: J. B. Lippincott, 1971.

Seraph on the Suwanee. New York: Charles Scribner's Sons, 1948. Reprinted, Ann Arbor, Mich.: University Microfilms, 1971. Reprinted, New York: AMS Press, 1974.

2. Other Publications

(For a more complete bibliography, see Robert Hemenway, "Appendix," *Zora Neale Hurston: A Literary Biography*, 1977.)

"John Redding Goes to Sea." *Stylus* 1 (May 1921): 11–22. Reprinted in *Opportunity* 4 (January 1926): 16–21.

"Drenched in Light." *Opportunity* 2 (December 1924): 371–74.

"Spunk." *Opportunity* 3 (June 1925): 171–73. Reprinted in *The New Negro*, edited by Alain Locke, pp. 105–11. New York: Albert and Charles Boni, 1925.

"Muttsy." *Opportunity* 4 (August 1926): 246–50.

"The Eatonville Anthology." *Messenger* 8 (September, October, November 1926): 261–62, 297, 319, 332.

Color Struck: A Play. Fire!! 1 (November 1926): 7–15.

"Sweat." *Fire!!* 1 (November 1926): 40–45.

The First One: A Play. In *Ebony and Topaz,* edited by Charles S. Johnson, pp. 53–57. New York: National Urban League, 1927.

"Cudjo's Own Story of the Last African Slaver." *Journal of Negro History* 12 (October 1927): 648–63.

"How It Feels to Be Colored Me." *World Tomorrow* 11 (May 1928): 215–16.

"Hoodoo in America." *Journal of American Folklore* 44 (October-December 1931): 317–418.

"The Gilded Six-Bits." *Story* 3 (August 1933): 60–70.

"Characteristics of Negro Expression." In *Negro: An Anthology,* edited by Nancy Cunard, pp. 39–46. London: Wishart, 1934.

"Conversions and Visions." In *Negro: An Anthology,* pp. 47–49.

"Shouting." In *Negro: An Anthology,* pp. 49–50.

"The Sermon." In *Negro: An Anthology,* pp. 50–54.

"Mother Catharine." In *Negro: An Anthology,* pp. 54–57.

"Uncle Monday." In *Negro: An Anthology,* pp. 57–61.

"Spirituals and Neo-Spirituals." In *Negro: An Anthology,* pp. 359–61.

"The Fire and the Cloud." *Challenge* 1 (September 1934): 10–14.

"The 'Pet Negro' System." *American Mercury* 56 (May 1943): 593–600. Condensed in *Negro Digest* 1 (June 1943): 37–40.

"High John de Conquer." *American Mercury* 57 (October 1943): 450–58.

"Negroes without Self-Pity." *American Mercury* 57 (November 1943): 601–603.

"The Last Slave Ship." *American Mercury* 58 (March 1944): 351–58. Condensed in *Negro Digest* 2 (May 1944): 11–16.

"My Most Humiliating Jim Crow Experience." *Negro Digest* 2 (June 1944): 25–26.

"Crazy for This Democracy." *Negro Digest* 4 (December 1945): 45–48.

"Conscience of the Court." *Saturday Evening Post* (March 18, 1950): pp. 22–23, 112–22.

"I Saw Negro Votes Peddled." *American Legion Magazine* 49 (November 1950): 12–13, 54–57, 59–60. Condensed in *Negro Digest* 9 (September 1951): 77–85.

"What White Publishers Won't Print." *Negro Digest* 8 (April 1950): 85–89.

"A Negro Voter Sizes Up Taft." *Saturday Evening Post* (December 8, 1951): pp. 29, 150.

SECONDARY SOURCES

BONE, ROBERT. *Down Home*. New York: G. P. Putnam's Sons, 1975. Discusses Hurston's short stories, placing them in the pastoral tradition.

————. *The Negro Novel in America*. Revised edition. New Haven: Yale University Press, 1965. Offers brief biography and critical assesssments of *Jonah's Gourd Vine* and *Their Eyes Were Watching God*.

BROWN, STERLING. *The Negro in American Fiction*. Washington, D.C.: Associates in Negro Folk Education, 1937. Terse, insightful criticism of Hurston's works.

BYRD, JAMES W. "Zora Neale Hurston: A Novel Folklorist," *Tennessee Folklore Society Bulletin* 21 (1955): 37–41. Points out how Hurston uses folklore in her fiction.

FORD, NICK AARON. *Contemporary Negro Novel*. Reprint. College Park, Md.: McGrath Publishing Co., 1968. Gentle, but serious, criticism of Hurston for ignoring the Race Problem in her fiction.

GILES, JAMES R. "The Significance of Time in Zora Neale Hurston's *Their Eyes Were Watching God*," *Negro American Literary Forum* 6:2 (Summer 1972): 52–53, 60. A perceptive reading of the way time is used in the novel to accentuate the conflict between puritanism and hedonism.

GLOSTER, HUGH. *Negro Voices in American Fiction*. Chapel Hill: University of North Carolina Press, 1948. Presents Hurston as a folk realist.

HELMICK, EVELYN T. "Zora Neale Hurston." *The Carrell* 11: 1, 2 (June-December 1970): 1–19. General introduction to Hurston's works.

HEMENWAY, ROBERT E. *Zora Neale Hurston: A Literary Biography*. Chicago: University of Illinois Press, 1977. Invaluable biography and criticism; chock-full of information and endearing tidbits.

HOWARD, LILLIE P. "Marriage: Zora Neale Hurston's System of Values," *CLA Journal* 21:2 (December 1977): 256–68. Discusses the idea of marriage, which Hurston allows a major role in her works.

HUGHES, LANGSTON. *The Big Sea*. New York: Hill and Wang, 1940. Firsthand reports about Hurston and her extraordinary impact upon people.

HURST, FANNIE. "Zora Neale Hurston: A Personality Sketch." *Yale University Library Gazette* 35 (1960): 17–22. Fond memories of an unpredictable, unfathomable personality.

JACKSON, BLYDEN. "Some Negroes in the Land of Goshen." *Tennessee Folklore Society Bulletin* 19 (December 1953): 103–107. Praises Hurston for her aesthetic achievement in *Moses, Man of the Mountain*.

JORDAN, JUNE. "Notes toward a Balancing of Love and Hatred." *Black World* 23:10 (August 1974): 4–8. Denounces the one-black-writer-at-a-time syndrome which allowed us Wright but denied us Hurston.

KILSON, MARION. "The Transformation of Eatonville's Ethnographer." *Phylon* 33:2 (Summer 1972): 112–19. Interesting discussion of Hurston's change from ethnographic artist to critical ethnographer.

KUNITZ, STANLEY J. and HAYCRAFT, HOWARD. *Twentieth-Century Authors*. New York: The H. W. Wilson Company, 1942. Biography enhanced by autobiography.

NEAL, LARRY. "Introduction." *Dust Tracks on a Road*. New York: J. B. Lippincott Co., 1971. Brief, concise appraisal of Hurston and her works.

RAYSON, ANN. "*Dust Tracks on a Road*: Zora Neale Hurston and the Form of Black Autobiography." *Negro American Literature Forum* 7 (Summer 1973): 39. Sees Hurston's work as a "paradox among American black autobiographers."

————. "The Novels of Zora Neale Hurston." *Studies in Black Literature* 5:3 (Winter 1974): 1–10. General introduction to the themes found in the fiction.

SOUTHERLAND, ELLEASE. "The Novelist-Anthropologist's Life/Works." *Black World* 23:10 (August 1974): 20–30. General introduction to Hurston and her works.

TURNER, DARWIN. *In a Minor Chord*. Carbondale: Southern Illinois University Press, 1971. Unsympathetic reading of Hurston and her works which nevertheless recognizes her value as novelist.

WALKER, ALICE. "In Search of Zora Neale Hurston." *Ms. Magazine*, March 1975, pp. 74–79, 85–89. Chronicles Walker's trek to Florida to place a marker on Hurston's unmarked grave; interspersed with a running commentary by Robert Hemenway.

WALKER, S. JAY. "Zora Neale Hurston's *Their Eyes Were Watching God*: Black Novel of Sexism." *Modern Fiction Studies* 20 (1974–5): 519–27. Points out that the novel, which is all about sexism, anticipates the feminist movement.

Index

Boas, Franz, 19-20, 21
Bone, Robert, 15, 56, 71, 98, 133, 171

Cunard, Nancy, 32

Ellison, Ralph, 56-57, 72, 132

Fire! !, 57, 58
Ford, Nick Aaron, 76, 171

Giles, James, 98, 107, 112
Green, Paul, 39

Harlem Renaissance, 18, 57, 70
Hemenway, Robert, 17, 20, 39, 54, 55, 62, 68, 91, 92, 94, 98, 114-15, 121-22, 133, 146, 164, 168-69, 172-73
Hoodoo, Voodoo, 24, 40, 153-54, 158-59
Hughes, Langston, 18, 20, 22, 28-31
Hurst, Fanny, 19, 36, 54, 57-58, 162, 167-68, 175
Hurston, John, 13, 14, 15, 16, 27, 90-91, 161-62, 163, 166
Hurston, Zora Neale: arrested, 47-48; birth, 13, 161; childhood, 14-16, 61-62, 161; contract with Charlotte Osgood Mason, 22-23; early failures as writer, 24-27; education: elementary, 15, high school, 17, college, 17-18, 19, 58, 162, graduate school, 35-36; fellowships: Carter G. Woodson Foundation Fellowship, 21, Rosenwald Foundation Fellowship, 35, Guggenheim Foundation Fel-

190

lowship, 37; first marriage, 17; involvement with hoodoo (voodoo), 24, 40, 153-54, 158-59; on her life, 55, 160, 162, 163; on her works, 39, 40, 46-47, 132, 148, 170; on 1954 Supreme Court Decision, 50, 166; on publishing restrictions, 33, 44, 50, 73; on race, racism, 33, 41-42, 50, 155, 165-69; second marriage, 40; Works Progress Administration Federal Theater Project, 36-37; Works Progress Federal Writers' Project, 38

DRAMA:
Color Struck, 18, 57, *64-65*, 135
First One, The, 58, *68*, 132
High John de Conquer, 43

MUSICALS:
Fast and Furious, 25
From Sun to Sun, 35, 36
Great Day, The, 26, 35, 37, 94
Jungle Scandals, 25
Singing Steel, 35

NON-FICTION:
"Characteristics of Negro Expression," 32
"Conversions and Visions," 32
"Crazy For This Democracy," 42
"Cudjo's Own Story of the Last African Slaver," 21
Dust Tracks on a Road, 13, 40-41, 56, 59, 62, 73, 90, 94, 117, 129, 148, 149, *160-69*
"Hoodoo in America," 33, 150

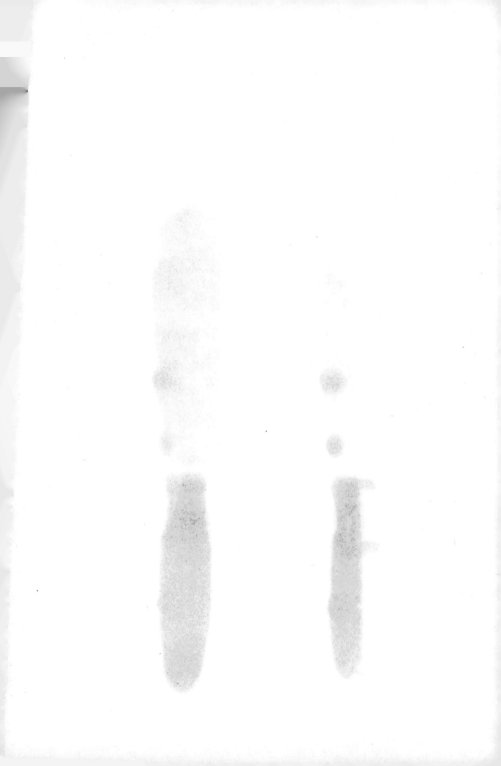

81989

HOWARD, LILLIE
    ZORA NEALE HURSTON.